HARNESS THE POWER OF THE INVINCIBLE MIND

SPATIAL STRATEGY TO SUCCESS AND HAPPINESS

D1259881

ALEX NEUMANN

Professional Editing by Cathy Suter
Cover Design by Ivica Jandrijevic

Library of Congress Registration# TX0008856980

Pearson press
sales@pearson-press.com

Ordering Information:
Quantity sales. Special discounts are available on quantity purchases by corporations, associations, and others. For details, contact the "Special Sales Department" at the address above.

Harness the Power of the Invincible Mind/Alex Neumann. - 2nd ed.

ISBN: 978-1-7771790-2-1(Paperback)
ISBN: 978-1-7771790-0-7 (Hardcover)
ISBN: 978-1-9992794-7-9 (E-book)
ISBN: 978-1-9992794-1-7 (Audio Book)

CONTENTS

THANKS

To anyone who is going through tough times. You are a real fighter. You are my hero.

To my beloved parents who did not raise an invincible mind.

To my best friend, my beautiful and kind wife,

who has to live with an invincible mind.

Alex Neumann

www.alexneumann.co

INTRODUCTION

Hold on to the ledge, whether it is physical or mental. If you are holding on by sheer willpower, determination, and stubbornness, that is enough.

Stretch yourself until your fingers bleed, your muscles scream, and your breath comes in ragged gasps, and then calm yourself, relax, stretch, take a deep breath.

If you can hold on one moment longer, and then one second more, you will find that the moments become seconds, the seconds add to minutes, and the minutes total to hours, until you have held on long enough to catch your second wind.

Then, with calm confidence, climb upwards until you reach the top.

Throughout my life, I have blindly fumbled upon stuff that I thought never existed. Sometimes I thought I had come up with a novel idea only to stumble onto a source that already existed many centuries before I was born.

Often, when I thought I was knowledgeable, I woke up only to realize that I was sleepwalking ignorant. I have realized that a lot of times, what seems to disturb us is not anything new. Life's challenges and adversities bothered our ancestors and those before them.

And so, why do these life disturbances keep on nagging our minds?

The reality is that there is profound KNOWLEDGE that, if we ever learned from it, would cause us not to be victims of violent disturbances, but instead would bring us blessed unrest.

We all have stories to tell. However, if you only think of your own story and never listen to other people's stories, such a monologue would be not only dull but also ignorant. Part of being knowledgeable is to appreciate that your story is only the tip of the iceberg, a small pebble in the ocean of human experience.

Knowledge is a collection of people's experiences and can teach us a lot.

Isn't that very same thing that we call "waste" what plants call humus? We are yet to hear plants speak, but when their roots dig deep into humus, their health and vitality speak volumes.

Well, throughout my life, I have fumbled upon the rich humus of knowledge and it has nourished the grey matter that extends my skull. I have extracted from it, rich content and distilled from it, a pure spirit that soothes my soul.

Do you wish to share with me this pure spirit?

Well, the old knowledge from China taught me that, "If you want to plan for a season, plant rice. If you want to plan for a decade, plant trees, and if you want to plan for a lifetime, educate your being."

There is a lot more that I have learned from other people's stories than I could ever teach from my own story.

In this book, I share with you such stories and give my perspectives on them. . . to make them come alive . . . like humus that comes alive in a healthy plant.

The knowledge that has lasting value does not perish. Herein is a collection of my knowledge. It is my distilled spirit. And it contains plenty of critical thinking.

I cannot pretend that I can teach you. However, I know that I can share with you my insights and perspectives. . . in the hope that you will be able to see the same darkness as I do and beyond it visualize the stars that I see.

Enjoy!

CHAPTER ONE

RIDE YOUR ADVERSITY

Adversity is the only love that will not be ashamed of you. Adversity is the best love that there is. Every loss, every heartbreak, every defeat has its lesson, its novelty, and its seed that raises you anew.

Through that adversity called famine, we learned how to till the land. Through adversity called a dry season, we learned how to store food. Through adversity called rotting and pestilence, we learned how to preserve food.

Through adversity, we learned how to build shelters, how to secure our habitats, and how to organize ourselves into communities and nations. Most nation-states were created as products of war.

Adversity is like that test of fire that makes fine steel. Without fire, there would not be fine steel. Adversity is what brings out the finest within us.

The main reason why we fear adversity is that it steals our comfort zone. No one would be happy if, all of a sudden, in the wee hours of the night, while we were deeply asleep, the mattress was pulled off the bed.

This robbery of our pleasure can create horrors in our imaginations. Yet, what if that mattress is bug-infested? What if that mattress is a borrowed one and the owner is simply, though rudely, taking it back? Isn't it a moment for a new beginning? Isn't it an opportunity to find an alternative? Or even own a new mattress?

Well, maybe this kind of rude awakening makes adversity, not such a pleasurable love. Yet, it is still called love. Isn't it?

Adversity simply has a unique way of expressing love for humanity. Therefore, we must find a unique way of appreciating its love for humanity.

Many times, we frown upon adversity. We perceive adversity as our greatest enemy. Why? Because it squeezes off the wound of our insecurity. Because it shines a light on our insecurities.

We desire to be soothed. We desire pleasure. We desire comfort. How dare you, adversity? How dare you prick and pierce my wound?

Well, if nurses pampered our wounds and doctors did not perform needed surgery, simply because they do not want us to feel pain, many of us would be dead.

What would happen if you refused to remove a child's tooth that ought to be removed simply because you did not want your child to experience pain? The child's teeth pattern would be distorted.

The strongest individuals are those who endured periods of adversity. They learned to cope with it. They become experienced at navigating their way through adversities.

Oftentimes, it is worth more to kiss adversity than to frown upon it. If it were not for adversities such as erosions, landslides, earthquakes, rifts, and volcanoes, the beautiful landscape that we tour and admire would not be there.

While admiring the beauty of the landscape, we cannot imagine the pain of the creatures that were caught unawares and buried or burnt alive. It is never in our minds. We do not even imagine that adversity took place, because the results are just too pleasant, and the pain on us extremely remote, if any.

We may think we are the most cursed human beings. There is a significant danger in listening only to your own story and being deaf to other people's stories. To understand, to fathom, and to appreciate adversity, listen to other people's stories.

No one wants to invite adversity. But pain and pleasure are what describe life. They are the hills and valleys that make a beautiful landscape.

Kissing adversity is not the same as welcoming it. It is merely daring it. It is to be ready for your challenge. It takes bravery. It takes stoicism to achieve this state of mind. Yet, nobody is born to be a stoic. It is merely a learned attitude. It is a created frame of mind.

Yes, almost everyone frowns upon misery, sorrow, and tears. Yet, there are those few, the chosen few, the fearless that find the moment of adversity so exhilarating. Why? Because they have had frequent doses of adversity, it has become their unlikely friend. They have developed immunity to negative reactions toward adversity. It is not that they do not feel the pain of adversity—instead, they have simply learned to overcome the pain and appreciate it. As soldiers, they consider it an endurance test, a hardening off, and a kind of prepping for a much more significant challenge.

It is common to find some people, who upon a small mishap, disturb the peace of others, thinking that they are the most unfortunate. And when others open their mouth, that's when they realize that they simply can't fit the bigger shoes.

Speaking of shoes, an old saying goes, "I cried because I did not have shoes, only to bump into someone who had no legs."

Some of the situations we consider adversity are simply not so, once we expose ourselves to the universe, learn from others, encounter their experiences, and hear their stories.

To understand your struggles, you must continuously seek and embrace the diversity of other people's challenges. Being consumed in the welfare of other people's adversity can help you appreciate your very own problems.

BE A MAASAI BOY

If there is one thing that combats fear, it is courage. Courage is the attitude that tells you "I can face the challenge and its consequences."

The lion is probably the most feared animal on earth. Yet, in Kenya, a Maasai boy can scare off a lion and even kill it if it does not get scared. However, in some other parts of the world, such a boy would be hitting the headlines of sad news, mauled to death by a lion.

It is not that a Maasai boy is stronger than any other boy. It is not that a Maasai boy has magic. The Maasai boy has been taught to be brave and he exudes this bravery through a posture that does not manifest any form of fear. Even a lion gets shocked by this rare quality of courage and takes off.

In the Kalahari Desert, there are menacing hyenas. The types that prey on children. However, like the Maasai boys, the Khoisan children have been taught not to fear or run away from hyenas. Instead, they have been taught how to overcome their disadvantage—shortness.

Generally, hyenas fear tall people. They fear heights. Therefore, what the Khoisan child does is simply to elongate his height. How? By raising a long plank over his head. This technique makes him appear quite tall. When the hyena sees a creature with this height, it gets scared and runs away.

It is the same story in everyday life. When people show cowardice, they get oppressed by Bullies.

Bullies, exploiters, oppressors, and other inferior beings have such a powerful ability to detect their victims. They can quickly tell a victim from afar. A fearful person is quite easy to spot. There are so many unspoken signs to see.

Like lions and hyenas, bullies, exploiters, oppressors, and similar types can issue threats just to see whether you are timid or not. If you get timid, you become their prey. If you become brave, they get scared off.

The same is the case with adversity. If you fear adversity, it will maul you down. However, if you are a brave stoic, adversity will become your shield instead of your attacker.

Stand up to adversity and stop fearing it.

There are those of us who have vulnerabilities; maybe it is a physical vulnerability such as not having a formidable body or somehow being disabled. Perhaps it is financial vulnerability such as a lack of income opportunity. Perhaps it is cultural vulnerability such as belonging to a minority group, etc. You can turn your weakness into your strength.

There is no greater teacher than nature. It's our job to discover and learn.

Trees don't speak but they can teach. It is a careful observer that can learn what the trees have to teach us (the so-called "most intelligent beings").

Buddha learned a lot while meditating under a tree. The serene shade provided by the tree gave him the perfect opportunity to dig deeper into his inner nature. He found wisdom under the tree and an answer to the question that greatly disturbed his childhood— suffering. Why do we suffer?

Talk about suffering and childhood, and that brings us to another person, not Buddha but well-known, nonetheless.

Unlike Buddha, whose childhood was blessed by the abundant ambiance of the palace, he had none of these. He wasn't from a noble family, but an ordinary working family. This boy was born the son of a peasant farmer who died three months before his birth. Thus, he never saw his father. His mother remarried when he was just three years old. This remarriage marked the beginning of the boy's miserable childhood. He disliked his step-father to the point of hatred. He began to have some enmity with his mother for marrying this man: Reverend Barnabus Smith.

The most probable source of his anger is the fact that his mother abandoned him, leaving him with his maternal grandmother so that she could consummate the marriage with the Reverend. To the boy, this was quite selfish of his mother. How could she abandon him and neglect him so that she could be married? How could she choose a stranger over him in terms of care?

The boy was so disturbed such that at one point he contemplated burning his mother and his stepfather alive in their house.

However, as fate would have it, after the death of his stepfather, the boy reunited with his mother at age twelve. Due to lack of school fees, the mother pulled him out of school with the intent of making him a farmer so that he could tend to the farm. However, the boy performed miserably on the farm. He didn't like farming. He found it monotonous.

Sensing things were not okay with the boy, the mother introduced him to his uncle for counsel. This brought him closer to his maternal uncle, a chemist by the name of Wesley Clarke. They quickly established a good bond.

The boy liked attending his uncle's chemist shop and thus gained a keen interest in chemistry. It is at this point that the uncle noted the boy's innate ability to easily comprehend scientific concepts. This prompted the uncle to recommend that he be admitted to Cambridge University after completing high school.

While at Cambridge University, he was taught calculus, but he became more interested in grander philosophical thoughts. This led him to create his parallel study to query and answer some of the tough philosophical questions of the time. His parallel study cost him his performance of the main course that he pursued at the university—calculus. Thus, he graduated without honors or distinctions.

Bubonic plague struck Cambridge. He was forced to go back to the village—to the very farmlands that he disliked. While sitting in the garden under a tree, an apple fell. Seeing an apple fall, this quickly triggered his philosophical inquisitiveness "why did the apple fall down instead of falling up?" It is from this falling apple that this boy "Newton" devised the famous Law of Gravity theory.

A boy who barely survived for being extremely underweight, led a miserable abandoned childhood, was pushed out of school to become a farmer, and eventually finished university with a not-so-impressive degree— got the greatest of life lessons, from the very garden on the farmlands where he was born.

This falling apple not only directed him to the Law of Gravity, but it also added sufficient gravity to his weight in the scholarly world. And by the Law of Gravity, Sir Isaac Newton was catapulted to the world stage. . . not just as a great philosopher but also as a great scientist. Don't forget that the prefix "Sir" connotes nobility. Yes, he was knighted and walked among royalty.

History attests that Sir Isaac Newton is among the greatest scientists to ever live. What if he had pursued farming? What if he had just focused on calculus? His fame came neither from farming nor the calculus that he studied at the university. His fame came from his "parallel" study that he conducted at the university— which never earned him any certificate or recognition.

Pursue with a zeal what makes you happy. Pursue with passion what makes your world go round. Yes, pursue with a gravitas that "apple" of your life. Cultivate an inquisitive mind. Do not take everything for granted. Whatever happens, dare to ask "WHY?" Only then will you be capable of learning.

Do not fear adversity. Embrace it and learn from it.

SHAKE IT OFF AND STEP UP

A farmer owned an old donkey. One day, while leaning in to get a drink, the donkey fell into the farmer's well. The farmer heard the donkey braying loudly and followed the sound to its source—and found the donkey standing at the bottom of the well.

After carefully assessing the situation, the farmer sympathized with the old donkey, but the well was deep, and there was no way to haul the donkey out of it. The farmer called his neighbors and asked them to come to give him a hand—and to bring dirt and shovels.

The neighboring farmers came, with dirt and shovels in their trucks. Neither the donkey nor the well was worth the trouble of saving. The only thing they could think to do was to bury the old donkey in the well and put him out of his misery. It was a shame, but there was nothing else that could be done. As the farmers shoveled dirt into the well, the old donkey was hysterical!

The donkey brayed louder than ever when the dirt hit his back, but the farmers kept shoveling. Then the farmers noticed what the donkey was doing. Every time a shovel load of dirt landed on the donkey's back, he brayed loudly —but then he would shake it off and step up!

As the dirt was shoveled down on top of him, the donkey continued.

The farmers and the old donkey got into a rhythm—the farmers would drop a shovel load of dirt down the well, and the donkey would shake it off and step up. No matter how heavy the dirt, or how distressing the situation seemed, the old donkey fought panic and just kept right on shaking it off and stepping up!

Finally, battered and exhausted, the old donkey stepped triumphantly over the wall of the well! What seemed like it would bury him helped him all because of how he handled his adversity. Instead of letting it bury him, the dirt became his road to freedom.

When a load of criticism, insults, mockery, and other cruel verbatim are being dumped on you, simply shake it off and step up! Do not let the load bury you in bitterness, disappointment, and crushing surrender. Instead, shake it off and step up!

Not everyone is happy to see you fair on well. It is human nature to feel jealous. It is fear of being left behind, being surpassed, feeling inferior, that breeds jealousy. This jealousy can be expressed in negative criticism, mockery, insults, and even harm. If you cannot shake them off, then you can merely step up!

Let your adversity be what helps you to step up to greatness.

Unlike this donkey, there are many people whose dreams, talents, and special abilities have been buried, simply because they gave up. They refused to shake it off. They refused to step up.

What many may consider adversity is the rarest form of blessing to a few. Wars make great generals, civil strife makes great leaders, calamities make great philanthropists, slavery makes great liberators, and psychological fear makes great priests. Every adversity brings forth the finest.

SEIZE THE POWER OF NO!

Make your "NO!" bolder than your "Yes." The greatest lesson we can learn from a doormat is its willingness to embrace every shoe. What happens to it? It gets a shit kind of treatment. It is the most preferred worker when it comes to sucking every sole's mud.

Fortunately, the doormat has no life. It is just a mere object. However, unfortunately, there are living beings that have allowed themselves to take up the role of a doormat for fellow living beings. And when I talk of living beings, I don't mean donkeys or horses, but human beings.

Why do some human beings choose to be doormats?

Well, early life experiences may have conditioned some people to self-sacrifice. What they perceive as a moral virtue of tolerance may actually be closer to a "doormat mentality."

Some humans choose to be doormats because they simply fear to say NO! Instead, they are saying "YES" to every request and command.

What addiction is to substance, codependency is to relationships. While not all, "Yes" kind of people suffer from codependency, a significant majority do.

Many human beings exemplified a typical doormat, a typical "Yes" sir/madam, until they regained their inner power to say "No!"

If you feel that you are often treated as a doormat for people so they can satisfy their egos, stop their shoes! Stop being available to absorb their muddy shit. Say, No!

From today onwards, start embracing this powerful word. Some people may call you rude; some others may call you uncaring. But neither be rude nor uncaring, but politely assertive. There is a big difference between being assertive and being aggressive. Simply be assertive without being offensive. Stick by your right to NO!

Gautum Buddha was sitting under a banyan tree. One day, a furious Brahmin came to him and started abusing him.

The Brahmin thought that Gautum Buddha would reciprocate in the same manner, but to his utter surprise, there was not the slightest change in the expression on his face.

Now, the Brahmin became more furious. He hurled more and more abuses at Buddha. However, Gautum Buddha was completely unmoved. Actually, there was a look of compassion on his face. Ultimately the Brahmin was tired of abusing him. He asked, " I have been abusing you like anything, but why are you not angry at all?"

Gautum Buddha calmly replied, " My dear brother, I have not accepted a single abuse from you. "

"But you heard all of them, didn't you?" The Brahmin argued half-heartedly. Buddha said, "I do not need the abuses, so why should I even hear them?"

Now the Brahmin was even more puzzled. He could not understand the calm reply from Gautum Buddha. Looking at his disturbed face, Buddha further explained, "All those abuses remain with you."

"It cannot be possible. I have hurled all of them at you," the Brahmin persisted.

Buddha calmly repeated his reply, "But I have not accepted even a single abuse from you! Dear brother, suppose you give some coins to somebody, and if he does not accept them, with whom will those coins remain?"

The Brahmin replied, "If I have given the coins and they're not needed by someone, then naturally they would remain with me."

With a meaningful smile on his face, Buddha said, " Now you are right. The same has happened with your abuses. You came here and hurled abuses at me, but I have not accepted a single abuse from you. Hence, all those abuses remain with you only. So, there is no reason to be angry with you. "

The Brahmin remained speechless. He was ashamed of his behavior and begged for Buddha's forgiveness.

SELF-LIMITATION

Most people underestimate the power of belief. The right beliefs are like having a pair of wings. Once you have it, you can soar over any obstacle and fly as high as you want.

However, the wrong beliefs can keep you chained to the ground. They will weigh you down and hold you back from doing great things.

There is an exciting story about a traveler who came across an elephant camp somewhere in East Asia.

He was surprised to see that the elephants were not in a cage and did not have heavy, cast-iron shackles to keep them from escaping.

All they had was a flimsy chain tied to one of their legs. These were large, magnificent beasts—if they wanted to, they could easily snap it with just the smallest step.

The traveler could not make sense of it, so he asked the trainer why the elephants didn't try doing just that.

The trainer replied, "That was the same chain we used to tie them with when they were still very young. Back then, it was enough to hold them. So, as they got bigger, they got used to having that tied around their leg. As far as they know, they are not strong enough to break it. So, they never thought of escaping."

In a lot of ways, people unconsciously shackle themselves to toxic beliefs. For one reason or another, these beliefs are planted like a seed in their mind, which continues to grow over the years.

Usually, these beliefs are tied to a series of circumstances and events. Or it could have been planted by people they met or grew up with when they were younger.

One way or another, all of us struggle with these negative beliefs that were planted in our minds at an impressionable age. The worst part is that they form a narrative in your head.

In small ways, you might find yourself unconsciously living out these stories in the way you act or make decisions. It could also affect the way you see yourself.

You might put invisible labels on yourself like "Loser," "Fatty," "Weirdo," "Mediocre," and other destructive manifestations of a poor self-image. The problem is that you do not give yourself permission to fully enjoy your life or celebrate your achievements because of these labels.

That is why the first step is to break free of these negative beliefs and your "story." And the only way to do that is to practice self-awareness and come to terms with the negative narrative in your head.

These narratives are tying you down, much like the elephants who are imprisoned by nothing more than their minds.

THE LAGGARD

Albert Einstein was something of a laggard in his early school days. Teachers said that he was not talented and not impressive. Einstein had difficulty speaking and is alleged to have only started talking at age four.

Yet, history attests that Einstein is one of the world's greatest physicists. He was a great genius in this regard.

Long after he died, many scientific breakthroughs continue to prove his theories were correct.

Albert Einstein did not let the label "laggard" torment him. He never cared about it.

In science, his spirit lives on. His mind is still immortal. What of the minds that branded him a "laggard"? They lagged behind the footnotes of history.

THE ACADEMIC FAILURE

Memories of the last century would not be complete without a mention of Winston Churchill, that World War II hero.

Churchill was a military strategist who navigated Britain to victory over Nazism.

If you were told that Churchill, considered a genius military strategist, twice failed the entrance exam to the prestigious Royal Military Academy at Sandhurst, you would find it makes no sense. Yet, even before this failure, Churchill did not seem brilliant since in his early life he had repeated a grade at the elementary school. He did so poorly academically that he was placed in the lowest division of the lowest class at Harrow.

Even in his first effort to serve as an MP, he lost. However, history remembers him as the prime minister who led Britain at the most challenging time in its history.

Before World War II, he had led the Boer War and made monumental blunders. He had since then been consigned to the tomb of the forgotten only to be resurrected by the devils of World War II.

He later wrote, "Never give in, never give in, never, never, never, never—in nothing, great or small, large or petty—never give in except to convictions of honor and good sense. Never, Never, Never, Never give up."

Winston Churchill is remembered as one of Europe's most important World War II figures. He was a great strategist, and this is exemplified in his powerful words, "I shall learn, and I shall overcome."

Yes, Churchill learned a lot through his blunders. And he overcame the harshest critics to rise to the highest political office in the land. "I shall learn, and I shall overcome," was proven through his deeds.

MISS THE 9000 SHOTS

"I've missed more than 9000 shots in my career. I've lost almost 300 games.
 Twenty-six times I've been trusted to take the game-winning shot and missed.
I've failed over and over and over again in my life.
That is why I succeed."
Michael Jordan.

The basketball legend, Michael Jordan, did not have it all glowing. It is hard to imagine that such a legend was once considered not good enough and thus was cut from his high-school basketball team. It is hard to tell how far those who were on the team went. But Michael Jordan's success speaks for itself.

If Michael Jordan had worried about being rejected as not good enough for his high-school basketball team, he would not have furthered himself in this sport. His talent would have been buried in the tomb of the forgotten. Probably, most of the world would not have known him the way it does now.

However, Michael Jordan refused to let this rejection bury him. Instead of being discouraged, he shook it off and stepped up.

TURNING TABLES

When it comes to the Davis Cup in the world of professional tennis, Stan Smith is a legend. He not only went on to win 8 Davis Cups but also proved his mettle at Wimbledon and the US Open. Stan is the boy that was once rejected in his desire to be a ball boy for a Davis Cup tennis match. Those who rejected him claimed that he was "too awkward and clumsy."

Being rejected as a ball boy and then ending up as a champion who is being served by ball boys is a typical example of "turning tables on one's tormentor." There is no better way to demonstrate that you do not care about negative criticism than to prove the doubters jealously wrong.

THE SOARING EAGLE

The story about a "soaring eagle" exemplifies its author—Richard Bach. Eighteen publishers turned down this great story before Livingston Seagull took it up in 1970. In less than five years, the title sold over 7 million copies in the US alone.

Yeah, the story of writers being turned down by publishers is almost a proverb. Yet, the story of writers who never cared about this rejection abounds. Many titles were dismissed by publishers only to prove the publishers wrong.

Thus, when your endeavor is overlooked as not being good enough, ignore this rejection. If you are confident that you have the best, do not give up. Keep working on it.

Keep improving it. And someday, you will prove the doubters wrong. You will have a chance to serve them your treat, and they will not match your fete.

HOPELESS AS A COMPOSER

"Hopeless as a composer" is what the music teacher called Beethoven. The teacher lamented that Beethoven preferred playing his compositions and handled the violin awkwardly. Yet, this "hopeless composer" wrote five of his greatest symphonies while deaf. How was he listening?

It is quite challenging to find someone who knows what beautiful melodies are made of who has not heard of Beethoven.

Had Beethoven cared about the "hopeless as a composer" label, he would have ended up fulfilling that prophecy. However, Beethoven stubbornly refused to accept it and thus proved the doubters wrong.

If you stubbornly refuse to give a damn to the doubters, the doubters end up being damned by their decision while you succeed. Simply, never give up. Shake off the doubters and step up.

Do not be angry at adversity. Smile it out. Laugh at your adversity sometimes. Mock it. Acceptance is all you need to embrace it.

The beauty of soapstone carving comes from the action of the rough agents that smooth it. If the soapstone carving does not go through this roughening process, it would not be as beautiful. We would never admire its beauty, for it would not be appealing to us.

Surprisingly, the same thing happens to humans. Most of those people who are humble, caring, forgiving, loving, and compassionate are often those who have gone through the agents of adversity.

Adversity trims your rough edges, such as arrogance and jealousy. It smooths you out. And, in the end, it attracts admiration toward you.

We know that the sunshine, which we love basking in every morning, is a product of billions of particles burning in immense heat.

We love going to the beach. We enjoy caressing its curves. Yet, these curves have been carved out and smoothed off by violent weather agents such as storms, powerful tides, and wind.

Thus, remember, whenever you see compelling beauty or success, it comes at a cost. Behind it, there are many untold stories.

CHAPTER TWO

DISENTANGLE

T here is no doubt that everyone wants to succeed. However, the term 'success' seems to have been baptized through the instruments of capitalism such that it has become, in itself, a market brand. A brand to be fought for in cut-throat competition through brutal toil.

As such, the pursuit of personal success has been trampled upon by the pursuit of "market" success. The market sets standards for this brand and fixes a price for it. Like any other capitalist item, its price is determined by the forces of supply and demand. The more people seek this brand, the more expensive it becomes.

Yet, like most capitalist markets, advertising helps to create a demand-pull, by inducing unreal and unnatural want for it.

Market success is hyped. Yet, real success is shunned by the market since it is simply hard to set a universal standard for it, and much harder to earn from it. It is so real and genuine such that the fake advertisements and induced demand cannot alter its worth.

An American businessman was standing at the pier of a small coastal Mexican village when a small boat with just one fisherman docked. Inside the small boat were several large yellowfin tunas. The American complimented the Mexican on the quality of his fish.

"How long did it take you to catch them?" the American asked.

"Only a little while" the Mexican replied.

"Why don't you stay out longer and catch more fish?" the American then asked.

"I have enough to support my family's immediate needs", the Mexican said.

"But" the American then asked, "What do you do with the rest of your time?"

The Mexican fisherman said: "I sleep late, fish a little, play with my children, take a siesta with my wife, Maria, stroll into the village each evening where I sip wine and play guitar with my amigos. I have a full and busy life, señor."

The American scoffed: "I am a Harvard MBA and could help you. You should spend more time fishing and with the proceeds, you could buy a bigger boat and, with the proceeds from the bigger boat, you could buy several boats. Eventually, you would have a fleet of fishing boats. Instead of selling your catch to a middleman, you would sell directly to the consumers, eventually opening your own can factory. You would control the product, processing, and distribution. You would need to leave this small coastal fishing village and move to Mexico City, then LA, and eventually NYC where you will run your expanding enterprise."

The Mexican fisherman asked: "But señor, how long will this all take?"

To which the American replied: "Fifteen to twenty years."

"But what then, señor?"

The American laughed and said: "That's the best part. When the time is right, you would announce an IPO—an Initial Public Offering—and sell your company stock to the public and become very rich. You would make millions."

"Millions, señor? Then what?"

The American said slowly: "Then you would retire. Move to a small coastal fishing village where you would sleep late, fish a little, play with your kids, take a siesta with your wife, stroll to the village in the evenings where you could sip wine and play your guitar with your amigos. . . . "

Real success is like water. It quenches your thirst. It sustains life. Yet, because it is plentiful, we overlook it. We are like the proverbial fish that asked its master "you keep talking about water, where is it?" and the master laughed out loud while responding "look around you, what do you see?"

Well, we seek market success just as we seek out oil. And like the proverbial fish, we ignore water. We put an expensive price tag on a barrel of oil. We fight for this barrel of oil at the barrel of a gun. It seems, to us, that this is the real success.

Countries with plenty of oil reserves are deemed the richest, regardless of the barren desert that engulfs them. Yet, countries with plenty of rivers that contour the evergreen forest jungle are deemed poor. Are they?

Well, the market puts a higher price tag on oil, yet, an almost zero price tag on water. Does it mean that oil is more valuable than water? Well, the market says so. But does life say so? What can you do without? Is it water or oil?

For thousands upon thousands of years, humans have lived without knowledge of oil. Even in the present day, all other living things, except the human species, live without much ado about oil. Yet, no living thing can live without water.

And yet, man's insatiable appetite for oil has created massive environmental damage that not only inflicts harm to his fellow men but also to other species that have no benefit whatsoever from oil.

So, must you sacrifice water to get oil? Must you sacrifice forests that brings you rivers so that you may gain concrete jungles fueled by oil proceeds in the name of skyscraping cities?

Why would a desert country with skyscrapers be deemed richer than a highly vegetative country with plenty of rivers and dense forests?

Success is evergreen. Like water, it is plentifully available. Yet, we scavenge underground for that which the market tells us is "success."

Within your very own nativity rests a great success. And like water, a REAL SUCCESS. Success is within. It surrounds you. You swim in it. Yet, like the proverbial fish, you ask, "Where is success?" You toil in agony seeking this market brand called "success." You sacrifice your very own real success to achieve that which the market tells you that you must gain in order to "succeed."

Do you think market success is worth worrying about?

In Africa, more specifically Malawi and Zimbabwe, thousands of acres of forests were cut down in the 1980s to pave the way for tobacco plantations.

The market told Malawians and Zimbabweans that tobacco is more precious than the richly dense forests that bring them rain, cool their environment, and avail them of plenty of flora and fauna.

Responding to the capitalist market, Zimbabweans and Malawians decided to cut the forest, kill elephants, lions, gazelles, and the rich flora and fauna so that they could supply this carcinogenic smoke (in the name of cigarettes) to the Western markets. Yes, literary cutting down logs for cash.

Now, is tobacco worth more than the rich flora and fauna? Obviously not. Yet, what does the market say? The market simply tells otherwise.

Real success is like the rich flora and fauna in Africa. Market success is like skyscrapers standing tall in the barren desert, thanks to oil.

Real success does not hurt. It enriches. It blesses. It preserves life, coexistence, harmony, and natural balance. Market success divides, displaces, brings chaos, maims, kills, and destroys.

We can witness the destructive wars in the Middle East, courtesy of market success. We can witness the hunger and famine that occasionally ravage Malawi and Zimbabwe due to market success. They blame the skies for not bringing rain. They extend begging bowls to the Western capitals to feed their populations—they are the victims of the very pursuit of market success.

Market success is actively destroying the ozone layer. Market success is causing global warming. Market success is actively spreading cancer. Market success has led to millions of deaths around the world. Market success has caused untold pain and suffering. It has made a few billionaires and dumped billions of poor souls into the dungeons of servitude. They are not poor because they lack money. No! They are poor simply because, like the proverbial fish, they are ignorant of the plenty of success surrounding them. They are exploited, and it is hard for them to escape this exploitation.

Market success has plundered real success. It has maimed real success. It has created desperate populations. It has increased the rates of poverty, crime, destitution, prostitution, murder, and suicide. Is this really success? No! But what does the market tell you? The market still shouts otherwise.

GREED DISGUISED

In a capitalistic sense, whenever one talks about the market, competition is presumed. A capitalist market cannot exist in the absence of competition. Sellers compete against sellers for buyers, and buyers compete against buyers for sellers. As in a tug of war, the price goes toward the one with a stronger financial muscle.

Yet, when a seller tramples other sellers in a bid to "win" a client, that is greed. When a buyer tramples upon other buyers to "win" a bid, that is still greed. This "win" cannot be a success but simply an illusion of it.

And yet, market success rewards these "winners." It does not matter whom you trampled upon so that you could "win." It matters only that you have not been caught violating the law. Even if it means killing, even if it means swindling, even if it means corrupting, whatever it means, and whatever it takes to "win," the market will ululate about your "heroism" and "success."

You will be invited to give "lectures" and "advise" others about "success." You will have bankrupt minds competing for your attention as their "role model." Like pigs elongating their snouts to sniff in the stench of rot, they will seek you out in the most daring of shameful ways.

Why? Because they, too, have been intoxicated by this fallacy of success. They have been taught about it in school. They have been incited about it in the media. Politicians and religious merchants have praised it, even though the latter does it with a pretentious disdain.

Money! Money! Money! . . . the new standard of measuring success. The more you have it, the more you are "successful." Lazy minds do not bother to investigate and search out the truth behind the facades of this success. Why? Just as an addict will not bother to find out where the drug peddler gets his supply, lest the peddler get angered and hoard it, they too have no interest in digging down to find the source of this "success." All they are interested in is hearing about the potency of this "success."

And even if some could ponder and think, they simply "have no time" to do so. Their labor is pegged to hours. And their meals pegged to labor-hours. So, they have to toil to accumulate these labor-hours in sufficient quantities to earn their daily bread, and feel that they are getting a richer share of this market success. They are lost in the noise of daily market activity with hardly any time left to rest their minds for critical thought. Is this deliberate? Well, the market system is set up in such a way that it turns humans into zombified robots, sweat machines.

Who are you in this whole facade of success? Like the proverbial fish, you and I are in it. I do not condemn capitalism. I don't hate capitalism. It is nothing but a system.

What is important is to learn what market success is—just an illusion. And thus, stop caring about the advertised gurus of success, the fake prosperity gospel, and other such mental traps.

Participate in capitalism, knowing what it is, for everything is perfect, just as you are. Participate in it understanding the role you are playing and its rewards without being ensnared by romanticized "market success." If you have got to earn your daily bread, please do, but do not expect the source of that earning to be the very same source of success and happiness. Success is within. That which rests outside is a market illusion.

The market teaches us that without competition, there is no success. It begins with the "education" market in schools. It flows into the labor market, and eventually into the "leadership" market that is our politics.

Schooled fools scoring the highest grade in the market education is almost a proverb. The darndest politicians scaling the highest rung on the ladder of society's leadership are a new inspiration.

The fallacy that competition boosts quality has become legion. Yet, market failures are pretty evident. Be it in schools, be it in the labor markets, be it in the national leadership, or be it in whatever market condition, the failures are self-evident. Yet, these failures are baptized with the "success" label. Why so?

Because the market keeps churning out lazy minds that are now baptized as "smart" minds. Yes, those minds that have to learn the art of conformity, the art of compromise, the art of playing dirty in a pigsty, the art of peeing the farthest and farting the loudest. Yes, the art of competing for the title of the most mediocre.

Is it a surprise that the dumbest actors becoming presidents has become the new norm? Demagoguery is the new norm. Fascists, Nazis, racists, chauvinists, sexual harassers, and other such dehumanizing malfeasants have been planted into the highest offices, albeit, in disguise.

Has our society lost its values? Has our society lost its shame? Yes! Whenever a society runs away from genuine success in the pursuit of market success, such become its value. Such becomes its shamelessness.

Let's pause and think for a moment,

Can one enjoy true success? Why not? Real success comes from enlightenment. It comes from true education. Unfortunately, the moment we sold true education to the market is the very moment we lost it. What we get is adulterated education, a poor education, a market education.

Market education is driven by the premium on labor. A premium based on market success and not real success.

The highest-paid in the labor market is one who has stopped pursuing genuine success and instead has gone miles in the journey of pursuing market success—an illusion.

If market success is akin to the destruction of genuine success, then, what is the market rewarding for its market education? The answer is pretty obvious. . . . destruction.

The real essence of our being is getting destroyed. Like the destruction of the forest to pave the way for tobacco plantations. Our true essence is being demolished to pave the way for the fake market essence.

For as long as we do not realize the destructive effects of market success, we shall never enjoy real success.

The enjoyment of real success is the realization that market success is a fake success.

For now, You cannot stop capitalism. It serves its purpose quite well. All you need to know is the purpose it serves, and what it is—merely a game. Play the game without becoming its addict. Play the game without becoming its slave. Play the game without counting losses. Simply play to enjoy. Do not give a damn about its gains or losses, they are a part of the game that makes it enjoyable.

Well, it is common for market advertisements to exploit human's desire to be free from pain and enjoy endless pleasure.

Yet, it is a fact of life that endless pleasure is only a mirage. While religions have traditionally exploited this unsatisfied desire by promising everlasting pleasure hereafter, the reality is that no one, not even the religious merchants, knows what the hereafter looks like. The only difference is that capitalists package this mirage of endless pleasure—here now—and offer unachievable conditions to get it.

Therefore, why must we be escapists of the here and now in the promise of the hereafter?

The "bitter" truth is that FEELING GOOD can only be momentary. Like a bubble, it is never meant to last.

Siddharta was a prince in an ancient kingdom in India. The king decided that his son would never experience the pain and misery that engulfed so many outside the palace.

Thus, the king provided the prince with all possible earthly treasures and pleasures.

However, like the proverbial fish, Siddharta grew weary of these pleasures. They started causing him pain. He desired to experience that which is beyond this pleasure: pain.

One day, he was able to achieve his wish. He went outside the palace, and that marked the beginning of a long sojourn. In this sojourn, Siddharta encountered the poor beggars on the street. This disturbed him a lot. In a bid to understand them, he became one. All in the hope that the "pain" of his weariness of pleasure could be relieved.

Like the beggars, he wore torn clothes. He slept on the streets. He experienced the meanness and sheer arrogance that beggars experience on the street.

He realized that he was not finding any relief to his pain.

He decided to go sit under a tree to fast and meditate so that he could receive enlightenment about the nature of being.

After so many days meditating under the tree, he experienced enlightenment.

It is only by going deep into the inner self that Siddharta found enlightenment. While the outside experience did not provide him with enlightenment, it helped him discover what does not work. If he had remained in his cocoon in the palace, he would have lived thinking that pleasure and enlightenment are only found outside the palace, the leeward side.

Even though Siddharta could have still found enlightenment while being confined in the palace, he could not draw his attention inwards since the noisy thoughts about what was outside the palace interfered with a state of rest.

Like Siddharta, most of us are obstructed by the market noise from achieving that state of rest, a state that can allow us to draw deep inside where real success resides.

Nevertheless, unlike Siddharta, who ventured outside the palace in order to experience this state of Feeling Good, most of us are fixated on entering the palace on the false notion that it is only within the palace where the Feeling Good can happen.

In our case, this palace is represented by financial wealth, big mansions, private yachts, private jets, exclusive clubs, etc. We desire exclusivity. To achieve this state of exclusivity, we yearn to climb to the highest level of schooling. We yearn to achieve the highest political office. We yearn to gain the top-most position in the Forbes list of richest people. This is the palace that the market promises us as the ultimate prize of its "success."

Yet, drawing lessons from Siddharta, Feeling Good is purely psychological. It is a condition of the mind, not of physical status. And yet, from Siddharta, we can draw one crucial lesson: that the greatest form of suffering is also psychological. Thus, both suffering and pleasure are domains of the mind. Market education will not let you know this critical yet obvious secret. But real education will never fail to present you with this manifest truth.

What brings market success is the ability to induce demand. Induced demand is not real. Instead, it is demand achieved by playing with a person's psychology. Due to human curiosity, there is always a desire to try out new things. This curiosity, in itself, is not bad. Curiosity ought to be encouraged. Human growth and development cannot attain a higher state without curiosity playing a role.

However, like a voyage to undiscovered lands, there is always a chance of getting lost. Many explore market success and get lost in it. They yearn for a return to their authentic self. This yearning for nativity causes pain and anguish.

This yearning for nativity in itself portends a discovery of true wealth. Once curiosity is satisfied, like that of Siddharta, you realize that you were already wealthy and still wealthy, but only lost. Through enlightenment, you begin the journey to discovering your nativity. When you are fully enlightened, there is no more yearning for market success. By then, you will have achieved true success.

As we have seen, media advertisements have the potential to alter perceptions. That is what they are meant to do. And they largely achieve that. Most of the indulgences we get ourselves into are driven by advertisements.

So, if you want to revert to experiencing genuine success, then, inevitably, you have to alter your perspective.

A perspective is simply the lens through which you see reality. If the lens is dark, you will only see the reality as a shadow. If the lens is blue, you will see the reality in shades of blue.

When you change your perspective, you change reality. When you change your reality, you can change how you perceive success.

What market success does to you is to commit perspecticide. It kills your real perspective so that it imposes the marketers' perspective in its place. Regaining your perspective means that, first of all, you have to become self-aware, reeducate yourself, be conscious of the various perspecticides floating in the market sphere, and keep away from them.

Thus, to end this perspecticide, you have to embrace self-awareness, true education, and conscious vigilance. Success can be defined in both qualitative and quantitative terms. However, a wholesome definition of success is beyond the quantitative; it is the qualitative outcome.

Looking at the definition of success, we can decipher the following four qualitative factors of success: compassionate service to others, a life fully lived, an achieved vision, and an eternal joy.

The quantitative measures do not matter, in the end, the vision is qualitative. It does not matter what you do, for, without compassionate service to others, there is no success.

It does not matter how far you traveled in your journey of life, if you have not achieved your vision, you have not achieved the ultimate success. It does not matter what you have achieved, if there is no eternal radiation of joy, you have not succeeded.

You can accomplish all the mechanics of success, but without these qualitative factors, you simply have not succeeded.

Let the quantitative be your measuring guide, but not an end in itself; for success is a distilled quality (like spirit) with properties unique from the raw materials from which it was distilled.

Maybe we can talk about transient success and ultimate success as a way of explaining success, but without compartmentalizing it.

Compassion is simply being fully consumed in the service of love, a love for your being and the empathy for other beings.

To be fully consumed means that you undergo full combustion of all vital energies required to bring raw passion into a fully consumable product, love. Success is a compassionate service to others.

You cannot be successful if you are not fully consumed in your endeavor. Yet, this consummation cannot make us happy if it is not for the service of love, the love of our being and the love of other beings.

The simple law of love is that you cannot love yourself if you don't love the nature of beings (others), and you cannot love others if you don't love your essence of being (yourself). Which of the "two" loves, comes first? Some sort of a chicken-and-egg question. Yet, start from where consciousness begins.

A life fully lived is a life that never escaped the plasma of existence in the present moment. It is a life not necessarily devoid of pain but full of appreciation for pain, which was the necessary and inevitable price for fully living. Success is a life fully lived, in the present moment.

Vision is not an end but merely a horizon that marks your destiny. Thus, as a sojourner, this horizon exists and continues to move as you progress until you arrive at your destination. A vision is not an end but the mirror of your destiny that keeps showing you that you are still arriving.

Can destiny be considered a fixed point somewhere in the future?

Well, just like vision, destiny is something you are still arriving at each moment you are on the journey. It is not a fixed point in the future, but a point that is still arriving in the present moment.

There is only complete arrival when the soul's purpose is fully realized. Like a river, a destiny is fully realized in its motion, in its arrival, and in its exhaustion.

Eternal joy is the glow that comes from full combustion. It is timeless, not in the sense that it is everlasting, but in the sense that it is fully present and infinitely present in the moment. The brightest moment of a bulb, lamp, or even firewood, is that moment when its energy (fuel/electricity) is consumed to the fullest.

Success is eternal joy, derived from full combustion.

We can consider transient success as that success which is achieved in moving from one step to the next, from the previous stage to the one following, from one milestone to another, etc. It is a transitional success, success in action, success on the move, a work-in-progress (WIP) success. Success is transient, and still arriving.

At the end of transient success, we achieve ultimate success. Ultimate success is the success of achieving your highest vision , your grandest state of being.

When we talk about transient success and ultimate success, we are not talking about different and independent types of achievements. On the contrary, we are merely labeling different points along the process of success.

Looking at these simple perspectives on success, you can realize that success, in its purest distilled form, is independent of the market forces.

Attitude drives your life. It determines whether you will succeed or not. To cultivate an attitude of success; see failure as a stepping stone to success, see failure as the process of success, a raw material that needs your ingenious ability to convert. See success as failure turned inside out, see success not as destiny but as a journey, and rise above petty jealousies in your circles that may dampen your spirit of success.

An attitude is a predisposition of the mind. It is a factor of one's mindset. Just as you can change your mindset, you too can change your attitude.

One great thing about life is that it is wholesome and perfect. Whatever we may see as its inadequacies are simply perceptive. It is like seeing the glass as half-empty while it is half-full. But the question is, why "half"? You can only see it as "half" in so far as your expectation of it is being full of water. But if your expectation is for it simply to be full, then having a mix of water and air makes it full. And, even having no water still makes it full of air.

Thus, life is like this glass. Whether your life will be fulfilling, half-fulfilling or empty depends on how you perceive it. Not what it actually is.

Maybe we can call this attitude of perception "perceptitude." Yes, your perceptitude can determine whether you laugh or cry, feel angered or joyful, feel accomplished or empty, feel successful or a failure.

Change your perceptitude, and your experience of life will also change. Remember, the experience is not what happens to you but how you respond to the happenings.

CHANGING VISION

There was a very wealthy man who was bothered by severe eye pain. He consulted many physicians and was being treated by several of them. He did not stop consulting a galaxy of medical experts; he consumed heavy loads of drugs and underwent hundreds of injections. But the ache persisted with more vigor than before.

At last, a monk who was supposed to be an expert in treating such patients was called for by the suffering man. The monk understood his problem and said that for some time, he should concentrate only on green colors and not to let his eyes fall on any other color. It was a strange prescription, but he was desperate and decided to try it.

The millionaire got together a group of painters and purchased barrels of green paint and directed that every object his eye was likely to fall on be painted green just as the monk had directed. When the monk came to visit him after few days, the millionaire's servants ran with buckets of green paint and poured it on him since he was in a red dress, lest their master see any other color and his eye ache would come back.

Hearing this, the monk laughed and said "If only you had purchased a pair of green spectacles, costing just a few dollars, you could have saved these walls and trees and pots and all other articles and also could have saved a large share of his fortune. You cannot paint the world green."

Let us change our vision and the world will appear accordingly. It is foolish to shape the world, let us shape ourselves first.

A good habit makes your work much easier to accomplish. To cultivate the habit of success, do not be a habitual waiter, don't encourage fear, be ready to take risks, and be prepared to spring up from a failure.

Success is not about the fear of falling. Success is about how you rise after the fall.

What kind of mark would you like to cast as your internal identity? What would you like to be identified as your soul purpose?

Not even identical twins are absolutely identical. Thus, each exists as a unique identity of what there is.

If the universe ensures that each one of us is unique, why do we violate the universal order by corrupting its intent?

It is a grand mistake that we have turned humans into objects of mass production for the sake of convenience, standardization, and exploitation.

We have uniform schools, a uniform curriculum, and the like. Why?

Children are born unique, yet, we will push them through the very same schooling conveyor belt. Once they pass through this schooling conveyor belt, they are transitioned into the classified employment conveyor belt, and their minds are carved, sculpted, and curated for the mass labor market.

By the time they are released from colleges and universities, their originality has already been lost. They are now processed and refined substances that lack a vital natural essence. They are simply not authentic but a replica of the mind-system that designed their molds. Why?

Simply because there is comfort in the average. Unfortunately, it is in this average that mediocrity finds its warmth.

Unfortunately, it takes time before one comes to the realization that his/her true nature has been destroyed by the system of averages, for the mere sake of ensuring the system owners get their way.

Some elements of this destruction are irreversible, yet, some can be reversed (not necessarily recovered).

The best thing one can do is to unlearn as much as possible. After unlearning, then, one can relearn through exposure, exploration, and discovery.

CHAPTER THREE

STOP WHINING. START THRIVING.

Often in life, we consider that which has denied us what we've been customarily entitled to, as an adversary. And the condition that ensues from the act of this adversary, as adversity.

And if we are not whining about the adversary, we are whining about the adversity.

A lot of times, if we cannot tell who the adversary is, we simply invent one to consider responsible for bringing the kind of adversity that we are painfully facing.

More often than not, we label this unknown adversary as the "devil." And by that, we start building a set of beliefs about the occurrence of this adversary. And we find a way of conjuring up a cause-and-effect relationship between this adversary and adversity. When we build enough body of beliefs, it comes to be our religion.

Take the example of death. When you attend a religious ceremony during a funeral, you will hear some people saying, "The devil has robbed us of an innocent soul." In contrast, some other group will say, "God has harvested his dues." In these two different statements, you find that God and the Devil are juxtaposed. And if you are curious enough, you will wonder, is it the Devil that has executed this robbery? Or, is it God that has harvested his dues?

Well, life is full of contradictions, at least in so far as our minds are concerned. Those who blame the "Devil" for the act of death are merely whining against the loss of attachment to the departed. On the other hand, those who are appreciating God for harvesting what is due to him are merely weaning themselves off the attachment to the departed.

Whining and weaning are a part of our reality. Just as we wean a baby from mother's milk so that the baby can grow strong enough to be free of the mother's breasts and get much stronger by feeding on other diets, we have to wean ourselves from our dependence on the "norms" so that we grow strong enough to face reality.

Affliction is one such opportunity for us to wean ourselves off the norms rather than whining about the loss of our attachment to the norms.

Affliction strengthens us. Challenges harden us. Affliction frees us from the stagnancy of business-as-usual.

ACTUALIZE

An entrepreneurial spirit is what many people admire but few have the mindset and determination to actualize it.

Being born into poverty can be tough. Yet, most self-made entrepreneurs were shaped, sharpened, and hardened by poverty. Many live desolate lives in poverty traps, surrendering to their circumstances, not knowing that this is the greatest opportunity to mold their clean slate. It is a taste of fire that makes steel fine. Similarly, it is a taste of poverty that makes a fine entrepreneur. Zhou Qunfei is a typical example of a self-made entrepreneur whose poverty conditions molded the best entrepreneur.

Losing her mother at the tender age of five, and having her poor father lose his finger in a factory accident and turn blind meant that Zhou had to find ways to support her family. She started raising pigs and birds for sale to earn some income.

Due to extreme poverty, she could not afford to finish her education. She dropped out and started doing menial factory jobs. Employed in a workshop that made watch lenses and did watch repairs, she performed her work with dedication. She knew that she wanted to start an enterprise and thus she learned as much as she could both technically and managerially. She even enrolled in evening accounting classes so that she could improve her record-keeping managerial skills—so that, when the right time came, she could properly manage her business.

Eventually, she saved enough to start her dream enterprise. Utilizing the technical skills, she had learned at the workshop, she started making lenses for watches. When mobile companies started replacing plastic with glass for mobile phones, she ventured into making glasses for phones and went further into making touch-screens. She won several contracts with both small and major smartphone companies—deals which catapulted her enterprise into a global leader in touch-screen manufacturing. The rest is history.

Zhou achieved her vision of success. Currently, Zhou stands tall as China's richest self-made female entrepreneur. Her flagship company, Lens Technology supplies Huawei, Apple, Samsung, and many other electronic giants with touch-screens for their Smartphones.

From Zhou's transformation from rags to riches, we can learn that poverty is simply circumstantial. It does not define your being. You were not born poor . . . only under poor circumstances.

Poverty is simply a "lack." A rich mindset sees LUCK IN THE LACK while a poor mindset only sees PROBLEMS IN THE LACK. An entrepreneurial mindset, like that of Zhou, is a rich mindset. A rich mindset is creative. Wealth is not in the things that you have built or accumulated. Wealth is in the mindset that you have created.

You can embrace a rich mindset. You can step out of poverty. Many have done so. Zhou is a living testimony. Neither 'weaker' gender nor 'low education' can stop you. When you have a rich mindset, neither of these exists in your mind, only in a weak mind's vocabulary.

One thing that holds many would-be entrepreneurs from starting up is the lack of a prepared mind. Zhou prepared herself early enough to become an entrepreneur. She acquired a package of skills that she knew she needed in order to succeed in her enterprise.

Out of the many skills she acquired, the most surprising one was training as a truck driver—a male-dominated profession. She knew she needed to perform any task necessary for her enterprise to survive. She was prepared to step into any position in her enterprise, and in the worst-case-scenario, do it alone. This all began in her mind. Acquiring skills were simply to actualize her mental preparedness.

Do not just save money to start a business, acquire critical skills that your business needs to survive in the worst-case-scenario. Being a lady, and starting her male-dominated kind of enterprise in such a patriarchal society at the young age of twenty-two takes courage and determination. Do not use your gender, age, or background as an excuse. Just do it—and excuses will step aside.

Just as it is hard for a baby to be weaned off the mother's breast milk without whining, it is also difficult for everyone else to be weaned off circumstances which they consider an entitlement.

Until we realize that we cannot achieve much without weaning off specific attachments, then we will not win anything. Weaning is winning.

It is by weaning oneself from the parents' nest that youth become responsible adults in society. They win their independence, autonomy, and freedom to exercise their minds to the fullest.

It is by weaning oneself from schooling after the final graduation that one becomes responsible for acquiring one's own knowledge, independent of instructions, and thus achieving higher levels of self-education. You cannot gain a career if you do not decide to wean yourself from full-time schooling.

Weaning oneself from attachment is the most liberating act of freedom. Weaning is the precursor to thriving.

ADDICTION

There is nothing that one must more strongly endeavor to wean away from than addiction. When the term addiction is mentioned, we often associate it with drugs. Yet, there are many forms of addiction that do not involve drugs.

Apart from drug addiction, we do have behavioral addiction. A lot of us are addicted to specific behaviors that we find hard to wean ourselves from. There are many kinds of behavioral addictions.

Addiction is a form of rigid attachment. We often think of addiction in terms of substance abuse. Yet, addiction is more psychological rather than physical. Thus, even in the absence of a material substance, addiction is still possible. The physical substance is simply a trigger.

Market success has become one of the leading forms of addiction in modern times. Not surprisingly, it is not considered a form of addiction. But, indirectly, it is recognized as a type of addiction.

For example, CONSUMERISM is commonly touted. Yet, looking keenly, those who indulge in consumerism do so as a means of displaying their market success—showing off that they have an enviable purchasing power is a form of behavioral addiction.

There is a lot of concern about traditional beliefs, and while some have chosen to condemn them wholeheartedly, the truth is that some established beliefs are indeed limiting. Yet, there are also those that are empowering and have the potential t to save humanity from the adventurous spoils of market success.

Thus, what is essential is to select those beliefs that help one attain the highest state of being while discarding those beliefs that pin one down from freely flying to the greatest heights.

While there is that school of thought that condemns the very concept of believing, the fact remains that it is practically impossible to find a human who is entirely devoid of beliefs. The very act of believing is not bad, per se. What is wrong is if the act blocks someone from reasoning, from critical thinking, from entertaining alternative thoughts, and from achieving the highest state of being. Real education is the best solution when it comes to overcoming limiting beliefs.

Traditional beliefs are of the past. Yet not all past is baggage. Condemning the whole past or seeking to discard it completely, is but another fallacy. We are who we are because of our past foundation. The entire notion of evolution is anchored in the past.

As such, it is essential that, just as we must have a critical analysis of beliefs, so we must also have a critical analysis of the past. Through this critical analysis, one can arrive at what works from the past and what does not work.

Thinking of the past, KNOWLEDGE ITSELF IS A PRODUCT OF THE PAST. As such, we must analyze our knowledge, and if necessary, put it to a strict test to determine whether it is applicable to our present circumstances.

While knowledge is a product of the past, it is still a product of the mind. To be able to have a critical analysis of knowledge, then, we must cultivate a mind capable of carrying it out.

One profound negative effect of overzealous attachment to beliefs is having a clogged mind, a wounded mind. Thus, to be capable of critical interrogation, one has to unwind the mind from attachment to held beliefs and attachment to held knowledge.

A great Japanese master received a university professor who came to enquire about wisdom. The master served tea. He poured his visitor's cup full and then kept on pouring. The professor watched the overflow until he could no longer restrain himself. 'It is overfull. No more will go in!' 'Like this cup,' the master said, 'you are full of your own opinions and speculations. How can I show you wisdom unless you first empty your cup?'

Through unwinding, one becomes an independent observer of beliefs and knowledge rather than a bound victim of them. Unwinding your mind helps you to overcome the obstacles of limiting beliefs and unhelpful knowledge that you have accumulated from market conditioning.

SHOWER IN CHAOS

Chaos is life's most exceptional brewer. During my early years of studies, as an introvert, I loved noise. I loved chaos, which often surprised my parents and teachers. How could a rather calm, quiet boy enjoy being with unruly groups? Why did he like noisy environments yet, most of the time, stay silent and calm?

I found comfort in a noisy class. That is where I could hotly debate issues. Maybe, it was a way of managing my shyness, for I did not want my voice to be heard.

Whenever there is a significant, sudden, and often irreversible change, chaos is often present. While many fear chaos, chaos is not necessarily a bad omen. On the contrary, chaos can be a harbinger of a new dawn, a break from the past order, the beginning of a new and better structure.

THE FAILED WRITER

In Yate, England there once lived a young girl. Her father, Peter James, was a Rolls-Royce aircraft engineer and her mother, Annie, was a rolling science technician.

Her younger sister, Dianne, was born two years after her birth.

When she was four years old, her family moved to a nearby village called Winterbourne.

She had been interested in fantasy stories since childhood. She used to dream with open eyes, write fantasy stories, and narrate them to her younger sister Dianne. Her early stories took place in nature, with trees, plants, animals, and children being the main characters.

She wrote her first story, "Rabbit," about a rabbit with measles, at the age of seven.

Later, she tried her hand at writing novels, for adults. But she never finished writing any novel. At the young age of eleven, she wrote her first novel—about seven cursed diamonds and the people who owned them. Her teenage years were mostly unhappy. Her home life was complicated by her mother's diagnosis of multiple sclerosis and a strained relationship with her father, with whom she is presently not on speaking terms.

When she was a young teenager, her great-aunt gave her a copy of Jessica Mitford's autobiography, Hons and Rebels. Mitford became her heroine, and she read all of her books.

After completing secondary education from Wyedean School, she failed the admission exams to Oxford University. She later earned a BA in French and Classics at the University of Exeter

A turning point in her life came while she was on a four-hour delayed train trip from Manchester to London: the idea for a story of a young boy attending a school of wizardry came fully formed into her mind. She immediately wanted to write it out on paper, but at the time she did not have a pen.

When she reached her flat, she began to write immediately.

As she was writing her "wizard student" book her mother, Anne, died after ten years of suffering from multiple sclerosis. She had never told her mother about her project and her death heavily affected her writing process. She channeled her bereavement by writing about the wizard student's feelings of loss in greater detail in the book.

An advertisement in The Guardian led her to move to Portugal to teach English. She taught English at night and began writing in the day while listening to. While in Portugal, she met Portuguese television journalist Jorge Arantes in a bar and found they shared an interest in Jane Austen. They got married and her first pregnancy ended in miscarriage. Afterward, she gave birth to a daughter, Jessica, named after Jessica Mitford.

She suffered domestic abuse during her marriage. Her husband kicked her out of the house at 5 a.m. one morning after they'd been married only thirteen months. Her child was only a month old when she moved to her sister's house in Edinburgh with only a suitcase and three chapters of her novel.

The couple separated. After the breakup of the marriage, she came under a lot of stress. She moved to Scotland with her infant daughter to be near her sister, taking with her the three chapters of her novel.

Seven years after graduating from university, She saw herself as a failure. Her marriage had failed, and she was jobless with a dependent child. She was diagnosed with clinical depression and contemplated suicide.

Signing up for welfare benefits, she described her economic status as being "poor as it is possible to be in modern Britain, without being homeless."

But she also described her failure as liberating and allowing her to focus on writing. In such a depressing situation, the only ray of hope was that she decided to complete the novel.

Her illness inspired the characters known as Dementors, soul-sucking creatures in her books.

While walking her daughter, she used to go to a cafe near her apartment and when her baby slept, she would sit down to write.

Finally, she completed typing her novel on an old manual typewriter. The book was submitted to twelve publishing houses, all of which rejected the manuscript. Everyone rejected the novel thinking that children's fantasy stories do not have the power to attract readers. But she did not give up and kept sending her manuscript to the agents.

A year later she was finally given the green light (and a £1,500 advance) by editor Barry Cunningham from Bloomsbury, a publishing house in London.

The decision to publish the book owes much to Alice Newton, the eight-year-old daughter of Bloomsbury's chairman, who was given the first chapter to review by her father and immediately demanded the next.

Although Bloomsbury agreed to publish the book, Cunningham advised her to get a day job, since she had little chance of making money in children's books.

The book "Harry Potter and the Philosopher's Stone" was first published by Bloomsbury Children's Books, under the name J.K. Rowling.

The "K" stands for Kathleen, her paternal grandmother's name. It was added at her publisher's request, who thought a book by a female author might not appeal to the target audience of young boys. Also, In that era, the chances of a woman succeeding as a writer were minimal.

Although most of the publishers rejected the novel, J K Rowling proved everyone's prediction wrong. It became very popular not only among children but also among readers of all sections. The Scottish Art Council was so fascinated by her work that she was granted a grant to write the entire series of Harry Potter.

The wheel of time turned around after that, the rolling of awards took place. Her thrilling novel Harry Potter & The Philosopher's Stone, decorated with 'Harry Potter' feats, has been included in bestseller lists on many literature charts.

The publishing houses that once rejected Rowling's manuscript started bidding to buy the publishing rights of her novel. The publication rights of her novel sold in the US for 1 million dollars. Such a high bid is rarely associated with any novel.

The novel became very popular. What happened after that is history.

Seven more novels from the Harry Potter series were printed and all the novels achieved record-breaking success. All the novels in the Harry Potter series were at number one in the New York Times Best Seller List. Rowling's novels have received many awards including the British Children's Book of the Year, and the Children Book Award.

Warner Brothers. bought the film rights to all seven of the Harry Potter series and produced six films. All the films proved to be very popular and successful.

Rowling not only became one of the world's most famous writers but was also counted among the world's richest and most influential people.

Rowling has lived a "rags to riches" life in which she progressed from living on benefits to being the world's first billionaire author. She lost her billionaire status after giving away much of her earnings to charity but remains one of the wealthiest people in the world. She is the UK's best-selling living author.

Time named her a runner-up for its 2007 Person of the Year, noting the social, moral, and political inspiration she has given her fans.

In October 2010, Rowling was named the "Most Influential Woman in Britain" by leading magazine editors.

She has supported multiple charities, including Comic Relief, One Parent Families, and Multiple Sclerosis Society of Great Britain, as well as launching her charity, Lumos.

NO ESCAPE FROM SUFFERING

The harder we try to escape from suffering, the more we experience it. It is merely because pain and suffering are an inevitable part of life. While joy is like a hill, pain is like a valley. Collectively, they do make a beautiful landscape. How boring would it be if the earth were flat?

What we must not forget is that experiencing pain does not necessarily result in suffering. While pain is an alarm, suffering is a reaction. We can experience pain without suffering.

We do not see the worth of pain and thus feel that the pain is unjustified. Hence, suffering is a reaction to unjustifiable pain.

The beauty of life rests not in avoiding pain and suffering but in confronting it, so that your life transforms into a magnificent landscape that fills friends and loved ones with awe while admiring it.

Do not just sit there mourning, weeping, cursing, and pitying your adversity; seek to get involved in other people's adversities. Visit a hospice, a refugee camp, a home for the elderly and impoverished, a disaster zone, and other such places. Consume yourself in the service of others. You will develop a strong sense of compassion such that you will see adversity for what it is—an opportunity to express sincere love.

Lord Buddha was on his travels to preach the new way of life. A woman was mourning her son's death. When she heard of Lord Buddha's arrival, she ran to him and begged him to return the life of the boy. Lord Buddha agreed but said that to bring the boy back to life, he needed a handful of mustard from a house that has not known death.

The woman wandered from house to house and found that death had touched every house and family in some form or other. She came back to Lord Buddha and said that she understood what Lord Buddha wanted to teach her.

Death is a universal truth and no one can escape its clutches. The only thing one can do is to pray for the peace of the souls that have departed. Sorrow befalls everyone. One must have the courage and move forward.

CHAPTER FOUR

INTENT . TIMEFRAME . EFFORT

There is no denying that affliction hurts, just as love hurts sometimes. It is intensified when there is a conflict between reality and expectations. When we build castles of hope in the air, we are more likely to fall into the depth of despair when life's storms hit hard.

A combination of high expectations and high hopes can be toxic. Yes, an excess of something is poisonous.

To unwind our mind from being entangled in the hurts of life, we must, as a first step, make a bold decision to face the pain of unwinding. It is from this bold decision that the other steps unravel.

Life is about choices. Every moment there is a choice to make—to wake up or not, to breathe or not, to eat or not, to go to work or not, to go to school or not, among so many others.

Forget about the common misstatement "I have no choice"! There is no situation where you have no choice. Every situation brings a choice. Maybe the options aren't so appealing or desirable, but there is a choice nonetheless. Without choices, there is no life. Yet, every decision has a consequence.

The three critical ingredients that characterize a choice are the intent, timeframe, and effort.

INTENT

There is no choice without an intent/purpose. What is your intention in making a particular choice? That determines the value that you have decided to assign your choice.

For example, you can choose to snap out of endlessly mourning your loved one, or you can choose to steep yourself in the depth of mourning, continuing to dig into it more and more every passing day until your life ceases to be.

TIMEFRAME

Every choice must be made within a specific time frame. Time is limitless. It is only a "frame" of it that you have cut out that is limited. For a decision to be termed as a decision, it must have a time frame within which it has to be implemented.

For example, when do you decide to get over a divorce? To get over the death of a loved one? You can choose to procrastinate as you wait for the event to happen by itself miraculously, or you can make a bold decision to get over it right now, in this present moment! Life continues to hurt the moment you prolong your bad situation with procrastination.

EFFORT

An effort is an energy in action that is driven toward the achievement of a particular specific intent. The energy that is not driven toward a particular purpose is not effort but wasted energy.

Whenever there is effort, it is always driven toward a countering force—inertia. It is only after there is enough force to overcome the inertia that things start moving from potential (stagnant energy) to kinetic (energy in action).

Yes, your world starts moving the moment you overcome your inertia (procrastination, dwelling in the past, exploring your pain, etc.). The same applies to suffering. Life hurts for as long as you do not put effort into pushing away from a hurtful situation. It is like a heavy object that has fallen on your foot; you have a choice to leave it there or drive it out. Both ways, you experience pain, but acting to remove the object is the beginning of the end of suffering.

A bold decision is one where the various elements of choice are fully optimized. Yes, the decision is most effective when the intent is the most supreme of them all (with the highest possible opportunity cost), the timeframe is of utmost priority, and the effort is fully dedicated.

Our modern lifestyle has brought us the misconception that bigger is better. Thus, we focus on grandiose schemes to the detriment of small details that would actually add more value to our lifestyle and bring forth the grandest way of being. Life is an art, and art rests in the finer details.

It is the little decisions we make every day that will either bring us closer to our goals or further away from them. Be mindful of the choices you are making when going through a difficult time.

If your goal is to move through the pain of life and come out the other side with your head held high, then, your choices will come down to simple things like going for a walk, taking up a new hobby, accepting friend's requests to catch up, going to bed early and getting sleep, and deciding not to inadvertently assign time to your trauma however pricking it is. This is the best way to snap out of it. Starve your misery of time and energy.

It all starts with a very minor decision such as making a call to a colleague; visiting a loved one; deciding to play with and entertain a neighbor's kid; taking a dog for a walk; deciding to teach some kids a music or art lesson; deciding to enroll in a charity, community mobilization, or relief organization, visiting a hospice or home for the destitute, etc.

Opportunities are all over for you to start small and grow big. So, do not think you must make a big decision in order to get out of a painful situation. Tiny bold choices can have a giant effect, just like a persistent small axe felling a giant tree.

Sometimes we consider a grand car to be more important than a great meal; a great meal to be more important than clean drinking water; clean drinking water to be more important than a fresh breath of air, and a fresh breath of air to be much more critical than sunlight. Well, which one ranks highest in order of priority?

First and foremost, without sunlight, the universe as we know it would probably not exist. Without air, life would not be sustainable on earth. Without water, we could not live very long. Without these things, our dream of owning a grand car would not come to fruition. Do we take time to realize that the grandest is in the smallest? All we need is to become self-aware! —An awakening of consciousness.

Why do we obstruct sunlight for the grandeur of skyscrapers? Why do we then pollute the air for the sake of our grand cars and big factories? Why do we pollute our drinking water with factory waste to manufacture cigarettes and guns? Why do we cut trees for the sake of tobacco plantations?

In all these ways, we can see that our little everyday decisions to ignore the most important for the sake of the grandest, cause disasters to our lifestyles.

In getting awakened to the consciousness of our being, we can get back to the basics of what is essential— breathing is more important than driving a Ferrari. Just enjoying morning sunlight is much more important than closing yourself indoors to mourn the death of a loved one. Just watching the marvelous patterns of clouds in the sky is much more critical than pricking the traumatic pains in our hearts. Isn't it? It is, but only when we gain the willpower to detach ourselves from our very own misery—unwarranted attachments that cause suffering in our lives.

What would happen if you make the small decision that every morning, no matter your schedule of work or study, you must have sufficient sunlight exposure?

What would happen if you make a small decision that better a small house surrounded by a natural environment than a grand house in a concrete jungle?

What would happen if you make the small decision that instead of smoking tobacco or buying products from water and air-polluting factories, you will instead enjoy some wild fruits and vegetables? The world would start to be transformed!

You are the world, and without you, it cannot exist! Your decision, no matter how small it is, for so long as it is for the greater good, will contribute to a world-changing transformation.

When life hurts, do not continue on the same path. Seek to make your life better. Eventually, you will discover a healing remedy for your hurt. Nature is wholesome.

Whatever little thing you do to make the world better blesses you in unexpected ways. What is the first and foremost bold decision that you should make?

INSIDE OUT

There was once a couple, married for many years. They were middle-aged. One day the husband, after a long debate in his mind, concluded that his wife could not hear as well as in the old days, so he thought she needed a hearing aid. Not sure how to address the problem to his wife, he requested help from the family doctor with whom he discussed the problem. The doctor advised him to do a simple test on his wife in order to have a clearer idea of the so-called hearing problem.

"This is what you have to do", said the doctor "Stay about 10 m away from your wife and, as if you are having a normal conversation, speak to her, tell her something, and see if she hears. If you do not receive any response then go to 8 m away, then to 5 m, and so on until you get an answer."

In the evening the husband positioned himself near the kitchen where the distance from his wife was about 10 m, and he asked her in a normal tone:

– Honey, what's for dinner?

But he received no response. So, the husband moved closer, this time in the door that separated the living room at about 8 m from his wife.

He asked again:

– Honey, what's for dinner?

Still, no response received. He went and sat down at the kitchen table in the dining area which was 5 m from his wife. He asked again with the same tone:

-Honey, what's for dinner?

Again, he received no response, so he advanced to 2 m from his wife repeating the phrase:

-Honey, what's for dinner?

Again, he received no response. So he went near her and behind her ear said with the same tone:

-Honey, what's for dinner?

– James, for the fifth time, I said that we're having baked chicken.

Before you find the problem in others, try and identify it in yourself. Sometimes the problem might not be with others as we want to believe, but inside of us instead.

Understanding your mind is not only the first and foremost bold decision you can make but also the beginning of a journey into self-discovery. It is a journey akin to that of a diver going undersea to discover the new world beneath the water's surface or of an astronaut endeavoring to discover the marvelous heavens in the space beyond the earth. It is a paradigm shift in the search for knowledge and discovery.

Yet, unlike discovering the treasure hidden within the ocean or the new heavens in outer space, understanding your mind is a journey inward. It is a journey that you can make an effort and travel toward. But, since curiosity has never met you to ask you what rests beyond your conscious horizon, you've never attempted to go beyond the conscious village that is within your mind. And probably, you have never tried to scratch beneath the surface to discover the hidden treasures below where you stand. Have you?

It is commonly said that experience is not what happens to you, but how you respond to life's events. This response will determine whether you will lead a life of suffering or not. Yet, this response is a product of your very own mind. The key to unlocking yourself from a painful life rests deep in your mind.

Learn your mind's ecosystem so that you may understand your being. There is always debate and confusion about the mind and brain. A lot of people consider them to be the same. However, using various analogies, it is possible to have a better perspective on the difference between the two.

The best analogy for the brain and mind is that of a computer: the brain is the hardware (precisely, the CPU), while the mind is the software. You know that without the software, the hardware is like a useless box. Yet, without the hardware, the software cannot function—it simply remains a concept.

Thus, both the brain and mind depend on each other; they are symbiotically interdependent.

Your brain is the most powerful bio-computer that ever existed. Your brain is comprised of the bio-hardware (the circuitry, the memory, and bio-software parts. The memory part is your mind has the bio-software part—your mindset. Your mindset is how you have programmed your mind to help your brain interpret signals perceived from your environment (both internal and external) and command a specific bodily response—behavior.

A brain without a mindset is like a computer without software—it can do virtually nothing! How your brain processes that which it receives (input signals) depends so much on your mindset. What the output of this process is (feedback) also depends on how your mindset interprets it. Thus, different mindsets can interpret the same brain output in different ways.

These different ways of interpretation are what we commonly refer to as different perceptions, different worldviews, different opinions, etc.

Other than the physical pain, emotional suffering is one of the most commonly talked about life injuries. More people encounter emotional pain than physical injuries. The most enduring elements of a life of suffering are rarely physical but emotional.

Your mindset can make you cry over the same thing that makes another person laugh. It can make you sad over that which makes another person happy. It can make you run to hide while another person confidently comes out of the hideout.

It all depends on how each person's mind is set! Have you heard a group of people celebrate the life of a person well-lived and thank God for harvesting his dues while some other groups of people mourn and curse the devil for taking away the same life prematurely? It is all about the mindset of each gathering of people!

We have heard of people who get hypnotized. Such people can be told water is wine, and they simply get intoxicated. They can be told that it is raining, and they simply start feeling drenched in wetness and cry for an umbrella. They can be told that the world is ending and simply collapse into unconsciousness. Hypnotism is simply the art of programming the mind to instruct the subconscious brain to respond in a certain way to external stimuli.

An old farmer lived in a small village with his teenage son. He worked hard in the fields and his meager possessions were limited. The most valuable of his belongings was a workhorse, which he used for tilling his fields. One day, the horse escaped into the hills and was seemingly lost forever.

The man's neighbors visited and sought to sympathize with the old man over his bad luck.

"We are sorry for your bad luck" They would tell him, shaking their heads in sympathy. The farmer, lifting his hands gently as if balancing a scale, replied, "Bad luck? Good luck? Who knows?"

Two days later, the farmer and his son were working in the fields. The sun was slowly creeping behind the hills in the distance. They caught sight of a horse cresting the mount. Their horse had returned with a herd of other wild horses. The son quickly corralled the horses and the neighbors were in awe of the farmer's good luck. He responded with the same reply as before. "Good luck? Bad luck? Who knows?"

The next day, the farmer's son attempted to tame one of the wild horses. As he rode in the corral, he fell off the horse and broke his leg. As you can imagine, this was believed by all the neighbors to be very bad luck. However, the farmer replied . . . "Bad luck? Good luck? Who knows?"

Several weeks later, the army commanders entered the village seeking every able-bodied youth they could find to fight in the war. As they came to the old farmer's home, they had no use for a boy with a broken leg. He was dismissed. . . . Good luck? Bad luck? Who knows?

Indeed, your happiness or lack of it depends on your mindset. Your joy or sorrow also depends on it. Whether you love or hate something/someone depends on your mindset. Whether someone will become your friend or enemy at first sight, too, depends on your mindset. Setting your goals depends on your mindset. Whether you achieve your goals or not also depends on your mindset. How you will respond to that achievement, too, depends on your mindset. Everything that you do and will ever do depends on your mindset! It is the key to your life! It is the key to setting yourself free from the imprisonment of suffering a hurting life.

CONTROL

In order to take charge of your emotions, the most fundamental step is to understand what they are, what their purpose is, how they came about, and how you can intelligently apply them to different situations.

There are things within our control, and there are things that we have no control over, such as the weather. People with mental health issues will often spend much time and energy on things that they have no control over.

Be mindful of the amount of time you are spending thinking about things that you cannot change or are unhelpful to you. For example, if you are feeling angry or sad about things that have happened to you in the past, this is not something that you can change. The past is in the past, and you cannot change this. Energy spent dwelling on this past is wasted energy.

When you try to control everything, you enjoy nothing. Sometimes you just need to relax, breath, let go, and live in the moment.

Do not let what is out of your control interfere with all the things you can control. There are those things that you can change, and there are those that cannot be changed. It is essential to know the difference!

Many times, we spend a more significant part of our lives trying to move huge mountains when probably what we required was simply to acknowledge and admire their uniqueness. We only needed to take a step to climb them, see what is hidden beyond them, and appreciate the panoramic view of that newness.

The fallacy of many of us is to imagine that we can endeavor to use all our might to change the world.

When I was a young man, I wanted to change the world. I found it was difficult to change the world, so I tried to change my nation. When I found I couldn't change the nation, I began to focus on my town. I couldn't change the town, and as an older man, I tried to change my family. Now, as a bedridden sick older man, I realize the only thing I can change is myself, and suddenly I realize that if long ago I had changed myself, I could have made an impact on my family. My family and I could have made an impact on our town. Their impact could have changed the nation, and I could indeed have changed the world.

You are the world, without which it cannot exist. Change yourself, and you will indeed change the world. It all begins with your mindset. Check your bio-software. Iterate through it. Test it, debug it, and retest it. If it is working perfectly, in harmony, and aligned with your highest aspirations, you will achieve that which can only be imagined by others as miracles.

The most significant determinant of what you can change and what you cannot change is your willpower. This willpower is fueled by a very powerful propellant—your ATTITUDE. Your attitude determines your willpower. Yet, your attitude and willpower are both products of your very own mindset!

There are several things that you cannot change. These include your past, your future, and people's perception of you.

Your past happened, and it cannot be changed. What matters, are the lessons you learned. Do not attach yourself to past occurrences but derive pure lessons for future applications.

Your future is not yet born. You are not sure that you will live it. Thus, it is good to plan for it, but do not let it sweep away your joys of the moment. Do not let it take away more than a fair share of what it deserves.

People's perception of you is not your problem. For so long as you are not alone, there will always be other's impressions of you. There is nothing you can do to change this, but there is everything you can do to improve yourself.

Just as there are things that you cannot change, there are also things that you can change. And these things will make what you cannot change less of a disturbance to your life.

You can change your attitude, your willpower, and your self-image.

Your attitude drives you. It is the ignition key to your willpower. It is the trigger that strikes the conversion of your potential energy into kinetic energy. And as your driver, your attitude determines the path you take in your journey, the speed that you pursue your mission, and the acceleration you have in your pursuit. Whether your journey will be safe or reckless, depends on your attitude.

Your willpower is the kinetic force that propels you to take appropriate action to change. It is your willpower that moves you from inertia into action. To exercise your willpower, you need the right attitude.

Your self-image is a reflection of who you think you are. Sometimes your self-image can be true or false. You need an accurate self-image for you to discover your real being, purpose, and aspirations. If you have a wounded self-image, you will see every challenge as a piercing threat to your wound.

One the other hand, if you have a healing self-image, you will see every challenge as an opportunity for you to offer a solution to the world. Do not let your encounters, your past experiences, and other people's perception of you replace your self-image with their self-image. Make sure that you protect the frame of your mind from being fixed in the negative image of other people's minds.

In the end, no matter how sweet your memories of childhood—where your parents used to pamper you and friends were genuine—that is gone with the past. You will never return to being a baby. The best you can do is embrace your adulthood and do the best you can with it.

You may have had a dysfunctional family, experienced cruel parents, and still carry the wounds of your childhood trauma. It is such a disaster. It is unfortunate. But, can you recreate your past life and correct the faults? Definitely not. Appreciate your pain. Yet, accept that bygones are bygones. It is time to move on.

You may have been hurt by your loved one whom you had planned to marry, but he/she eventually decided to marry someone else. He/she is happily married while you are still filled with pain, jealousy, and regrets. Just know that broken relationships are like broken glass or pot. No matter how much you can try to mend them, the cracks are permanent. There is simply nothing that you can do to reverse the situation. Move on!

Do not wait long at the closed door, for you may fail to see the new door of opportunities opened for you.

Everyone who seeks to sell you their brand of success will tell you that you have to rise above the average.

It is common for the average to be condemned as "mediocrity."

Many fail to comprehend the essence of life. When it comes to life, we only know its tip. The bulk of the iceberg rests deep beyond our comprehension.

So, why would we, with a simple knowledge of this "tip" claim mastery of the entire "iceberg"?

It seems like we all walk naked in the dark, yet, the little light that comes from stars make some of us presume not only our absolute knowledge of the stars but also absolute ownership of the light.

Yet, like death, we are not in control of when this starry light dim. So, are we in control? Are we really in control of our lives if we are not able to stop its end, death?

You are simply not in absolute control of your life. You are in control of specific parameters and a particular territory of this gigantic iceberg, its visible tip.

Do not overthink every little thing that comes your way in life. Sometimes, it is fair to mind only what comes your way.

WIDE-AWAKE

Focusing is a mental phenomenon. When you are mentally disturbed, such as when you are filled with worries, anxiety, stress, and even depression, there are plenty of thoughts racing through your mind such that you cannot focus on a specific thought that is of importance to your present needs.

Thus, the best way to be focused is to declutter your mind from these racing thoughts. A free mind is a focused mind. Yet, for the mind to be free, it must not be tethered to the past nor catapulted into the future. It must be open to the present unwrapping in the moment of now.

CIRCLE

"I am because you are."
The spirit of Ubuntu

We, humans, are social beings. Without social interactions, the worth of a human being declines to zero. This is why some lonely people race with suicidal thoughts in their minds, while some carry out these actions. Without others, you cannot be. Thus, to be a better you, to become all you need to be, you must engage the right associations. The greatness of a person is the association that he keeps. This is true in business, in politics, and in all aspects of life.

Thus, to engage in the right associations is to experience life's joys. To join the wrong associations is to experience life's hurts. The choice is yours! Make yourself happy.

Tell me your friends and I will tell you who you are. There is that kind of natural repulsion that happens when you try to engage in friendship with a person who is not a good fit. Becoming someone's friend is such a subtle natural selection that depends so much on your inner being. It depends so much more on your emotional intelligence than anything else. It is more of a gut feeling. When you try to force a friendship that does not or ought not to exist, life will inevitably hurt. When you allow yourself to experience the spontaneity of friendship as it arises, you will experience a happy, joyful life.

You are the company that you keep. Yet, friends are not just for interaction. Friends shape you and, in the process, you shape them. You become one in so many aspects. That is why it is easy to know and understand someone by studying the company that he/she keeps. Hence, if you want to be judged well, then, keep the right associations! To become a better you, a joyful you, a happy you, keep the right company, and surely life will not hurt, that much.

Your associations become your lifestyle. Without associations, there is no lifestyle! Thus, if there is a certain kind of lifestyle that you admire or aspire to have, seek association with people who are already living it. Work toward it. It is the ultimate wealth that you can ever acquire. All other forms of wealth will ultimately fall in line.

You cannot fake your associations just as you cannot fake your friendships. It can only come from your inner desire. It must be cultivated by the efforts of your emotional intelligence. Your associations are like stairs. Having stairs does not guarantee you get to the top; they only provide the ways and means. It is up to you to take the action of climbing to the top. It is up to you to marshal your muscles to continue climbing, resting if you must, but not giving up midway. It all depends on your will and power—the willpower.

Your relationships are a significant investment—probably the richest investment that you could ever have. Like any other intelligent investor, you do not want to keep dead investments. Investments that consume more than they bring are not worth keeping. Keep reviewing your relationships, and for those branches that no longer bear fruit, prune them, so those that do bear fruit are healthier.

Negative people are like a very low ceiling that prevents you from standing up, let alone jumping to a higher level. They negatively affect your self-esteem, self-confidence, self-worth, and self-actualization. They are a disaster for your well-being. The earlier you let go of them, the more you are back on track to optimize your potential of becoming all you have ever dreamt of becoming.

Life hurts when you are constrained. Frustrations are simply the energy of a potential that has not been allowed to actualize.

If you want to change the way you have been, then, seek changemakers in your relationships. Yes, people who show you a different perspective on life. People who see opportunities in what you can only see as problems. People who are ready to take your hand and help you make a giant leap over an obstacle, people who are ready and willing to go the extra mile just to make sure that you don't give up on your resolve. These are the changemakers that you need! Life will stop hurting when you embrace such people.

ETERNAL STANZA

Life is so simple; life is so basic. Yet, many of us waste it chasing glitter beyond the horizon. Do we have time just to walk barefoot on the grass and feel its effect beneath our feet? Do we have time just to watch the marvels of a waterfall and just be without thoughts ringing about our job, business, yesterday, and tomorrow?

The greatest of miracles happen not in great things but in the small things that we overlook. Just watch safari ants marching and building their path, guarding and ferrying foodstuff to their about-to-be kingdom. As blind as they are, they probably work more miracles than that which we achieve in bellowing factories.

The real meaning of life is not in the big things but in the small things that we so often take for granted. Life hurts when we take for granted things like just sitting calmly and taking a deep breath—playing around just to have fun—tending to a small garden in your backyard or an indoor pot. Spending time to fetch clean, natural, organic ingredients for the meal that you are going to cook, playing with your lovely pet, having time to play with children, visiting and spending time with your parents/grandparents, etc. It is these small activities that absorb the shock of life's hurts, leaving you to ride comfortably to your life's destiny.

A little girl lived in a small, very simple, poor house on a hill, and as she grew, she would play in the small garden, and she was able to see over the garden fence and across the valley to a wonderful house high on the hill—and this house had golden windows, so golden and shining that the little girl would dream of how magic it would be to grow up and live in a house with golden windows instead of an ordinary house like hers.

And although she loved her parents and her family, she yearned to live in such a golden house and dreamed all day about how wonderful and exciting it must feel to live there.

When she got to an age where she gained enough skill and sensibility to go outside her garden fence, she asked her mother if she could go for a bike ride outside the gate and down the lane. After pleading with her, her mother finally allowed her to go, insisting that she kept close to the house and not wander too far. The day was beautiful and the little girl knew exactly where she was heading! Down the lane and across the valley, she rode her bike until she got to the gate of the golden house on the other hill.

As she dismounted her bike and leaned it against the gate post, she focused on the path that leads to the house and then on the house itself. . . . and was so disappointed as she realized all the windows were plain and rather dirty, reflecting nothing other than the sad neglect of a house that stood derelict.

So sad she didn't go any further and turned, heartbroken as she remounted her bike. . . . As she glanced up she saw a sight that amazed her. . . . there across the way on her side of the valley was a little house and its windows glistened golden . . .. as the sun shone on her little home.

She realized that she had been living in her golden house and all the love and care she found there was what made her home the "golden house." Everything she dreamed of was right there in front of her nose!

Have you ever postponed that lovely stanza of poetry that just ran through your mind simply to be somewhere on time? Have you ever muted that sound of music that had started reverberating in your vocals simply because it was not the "right" time? Well, those were the moments of real living that you wished away as you were getting ready to live them later, only for the "right" time to come, and you realize that the poem and lyric have gone to the world of the forgotten never to come back. That's a piece of life that died with the poem and the music forever!

Opportunities such as these are plenty and come spontaneously. They knock quite often—it's all about how prepared you are to grab them and drink from the sweet potion they present. Life hurts when you miss partaking from such opportunities simply because you were not ready. . . . you were focused on the future or trapped in the past.

Carry with you a pen and a notebook. Carry with you a camera. Carry with you a voice recorder. These are the little things that you can carry around without feeling weighty, yet can grab great moments, and life-transforming thoughts. Yes, life hurts when you let opportunities fizzle away from you. Seize the moment!

Just as we keep away our poems and music, in the same way, we keep away our eternal life. A life not fully lived in the very moment is an experience that is lost to eternity. A poem lost is a poem untold. Music lost is music unsung. How else would we have impacted others if not through that poem and music? How would our loved ones be if they had listened to our poem and danced to our music? What a lasting inspiration would you have willed your loved ones had they listened to your poem and danced to your music?

Eternal life is that life that continues to impact your loved ones and others for years and years, long after you are gone. Eternal life does not depend on how long you live but on how much you transformed yourself to impact positively on others, such as to continue bequeathing a lasting legacy generation after generation.

Eternal life is one lived entirely in the moment of now. It is one that bequeaths others a legacy that is free from suffering and salvages them from their very own pain.

The fact that your coming into birth was an effort of many people and your very upbringing an effort of even a more significant multitude, means you owe your life not just to you but to many others—gone, living, and yet to come.

Live your life so that others may comfortably live. Leave a path so that others may have their journeys easier because you lived to create it. It is the essence of eternity.

LIFE is a dichotomy of two sets of words: Lasting Inspiration and Forever Energized. Lasting inspiration is that kind of inspiration that does not extinguish. That is, an inspiration that remains relevant generation after generation and its relevance seems not to have any anticipated or foreseeable expiration date. It is a healing balm to others' life hurts.

To be a lasting inspiration to others so that they too may lead a healthy, happy, and long life, you need to have a great lifestyle.

A great lifestyle is the best way to have a lasting inspiration. A great lifestyle is a lifestyle that enables you to have peace, joy, serenity, and be in harmony with yourself, the nature of beings, and the nature of things.

In essence, it is a life that helps you to be free from hurts—frictions, and conflicts with your nature of being and the nature of things. Such a lifestyle encompasses wholesome well-being characterized by the right mindset, healthy diet, regular physical fitness, productive relationships, and balance and harmony with the nature of things and the nature of beings.

EMOTIONAL EQUANIMITY

You can only love others as much as you love yourself. So, love yourself so that you're able to love others.

Self-compassion is being considerate enough to understand that your world flows from inside into the outer world. What gets out reflects that which is inside. Self-compassion is not selfish or denying others of compassion but realizing that ultimately, like that vehicle that ferries others, it has to be well in its mechanics to make the journey safer, enjoyable, and achievable. Thus, self-compassion is a kind of compassion turned inside out.

To practice self-compassion; is to be in love with your being. It is to know that without self-love actualized through action to relieve yourself of challenges and suffering, you cannot achieve the same for others. You have to begin from inside. You have to tend to your wound with tender love, and understand its sources and its eventual end. You have to heal your wounds. Only then you are able to do the same for others. Having self-love accompanied by faith in your being is the healing balm for your trauma.

A woman who had worked all her life to bring about good was granted one wish: "Before I die let me visit both hell and heaven." Her wish was granted.

She was whisked off to a great banqueting hall. The tables were piled high with delicious food and drink. Around the tables sat miserable, starving people as wretched as could be. "Why are they like this?" she asked the angel who accompanied her. "Look at their arms," the angel replied. She looked and saw that attached to the people's arms were long chopsticks secured above the elbow. Unable to bend their elbows, the people aimed the chopsticks at the food, missed every time, and sat hungry, frustrated, and miserable. "Indeed, this is hell! Take me away from here!"

She was then whisked off to heaven. Again, she found herself in a great banqueting hall with tables piled high. Around the tables sat people laughing, contented, joyful. "No chopsticks I suppose," she said. "Oh yes there are. Look—just as in hell they are long and attached above the elbow but look . . . here people have learned to feed one another."

The love that you give is the only love that you keep. Love is the fuel that drives compassion. Without love, empathy cannot exist. To be compassionate is to express love in deeds.

There is no way you can love others without first loving yourself. All else will be a pretense. Love radiates from inside to outside. Without it being inside, it cannot be outside.

When it comes to love and compassion, you can only receive as much as you give. Thus, if you have to love yourself dearly, then, you have to love others dearly. Self-compassion must, for its very own survival, be externalized into compassion for others. This is where it derives its muscular strength and fitness.

Self-pity, anger, remorse, and bitterness are all life hurts that are symptomatic of pain for that which happened in the past. They are signs of a lack of happiness.

You must own your pain. To own your pain is to accept that what happened is irreversible and had its consequences, which you are experiencing right now. You have to detach yourself from this sensitivity and experience pain for what it is—a crying call for healing. Focus on healing. The pain must not degenerate into self-pity, anger, remorse, and bitterness.

Life is tough sometimes. Acceptance of pain without reacting to it brings emotional intelligence. Treat yourself for ten minutes a day with a soft word, a hand on your heart, and a level of understanding that what you are going through is painful. You are human, and as a human, you will experience pain and suffering. If you try to avoid this emotional experience through avoidance behaviors such as drugs or alcohol, you suffer further.

FOREVER ENERGIZED

Forever Energized simply means that this Lasting Inspiration does not extinguish. It is self-energizing, generation after generation. It is an inspiration that, in itself, contains a self-propelled life force. Whoever comes into its manifestation gets energized by its being.

Those legendary personalities may have lived hundreds or thousands of years ago, but, from their histories, we continue to be inspired by their words and deeds. Whenever we read their stories, we are uplifted and energized as if we are getting words straight from their mouths and benefiting from their acts. This is only because their words and deeds have had lasting inspiration. And these words and deeds are forever energized by those who read about them and connect with their inherent power.

To be forever energized, you need to have a legacy worth bequeathing to your family, your community, your generation, and many other generations to come. That legacy should not be a transmission of life's hurts, but a transmission of the joys and happiness of life.

CHAPTER FIVE

RISK WHISPER

Failure is one of the most honest friends you will ever have. You may feel let down by everything else that failure whispers to you. But you will never be let down by the sheer honesty with which failure lets you know.

Failure will always be ready to teach you the difference between what works and what doesn't work. It will show you the facts from the fallacies, the reality from fantasies, hard work from laziness, persistence from giving up; there are many lessons that failure will always be honest with you about.

Unlike most friends, failure does not give up on showing you what does not work, until you find what works or give up on its friendship.

We have all failed at some point in life. Yet, we are still alive. Some of the consequences we deemed as horrible were not so. At times, we felt like it was the end of life, but this feeling passed.

Yet, even with such past experiences, we still fear failure. Why? Because we have been made to believe that failure is bad. No one has dared teach you that

FAILURE IS GOOD. Why? It is because society loves "norms," and anything that is outside these bounds is frowned upon.

While embracing failure, prudence and caution are the shields that you must possess. Embracing failure does not mean that you have to be reckless and careless. It simply means that you need to be aware of the risks involved, but they should not make you forego the big picture, the success.

Faith is failure-proof. While most people consider faith to be the domain of religion, faith is independent of religion. Faith is taking action without being distracted by fear of risk. It is being fully absorbed in your life activities such that there is no room to welcome fear.

Life is a series of risks. Risks are everywhere. Most of the time you go through them unhurt. For example, we all know that death hangs around us. But the moment you get entirely immersed in the fear of death is the very moment that you die.

If you fear all the risks to your life, you simply won't live. It is by faith that such risks do not come to mind. It is by faith that you do not even bother to think about accidents when you board a vehicle or think about an explosive inferno when you strike a matchbox.

Faith rests in pushing most of these risks to the subconscious. But there are those risks that you cannot push to the subconscious mind. These are risks that you cannot assume. For example, deliberately taking poison when you know it is fatal is a dumb risk—unless you have deliberately decided to commit suicide.

FEAR OF TIME

We cannot hold onto time. It is a phenomenon that we have created in our minds and attached to natural occurrences such as the disappearance of light and the fall of darkness, the departure of one season, and the coming of the next.

Day-and-Night occurs independently of our existence. Whether you are alive or dead, days and nights continue to happen. You cannot stop them. You cannot stop the earth from rotating around the sun, at least not yet.

These attachments are creations of the mind. Time is one such attachment.

And with these attachments, we have two days; the thought of them either gives us joy or sorrow. Very few of us can feel indifferent when Yesterday and Tomorrow are mentioned.

We remember our attachments to yesterday. And depending on whether we felt pleasure or pain, we will either laugh or cry, appreciate or regret. Yesterday is a creation of the mind. We can choose what to do with it. We can change it. You can change your yesterday!

Another attachment that we either look up to or try to evade is tomorrow. We look up to tomorrow when we have attached some likely pleasurable occurrence to it. Yet, we tend to want to avoid tomorrow when we have attached some possible painful events to it.

But when we have a painful attachment to tomorrow, we frown upon it. We do not even prepare to face it. We wake up to so many possible risks that will come with it. We get stressed out. We become anxious, sometimes angry, and even depressed, and at worst, commit suicide just to make sure that we never come to it.

Yet, tomorrow is only in your mind. It is nowhere else. Tomorrow is nothing but a package of expectations that you have attached to the next sunrise. You can change tomorrow!

Learn from those who never mind failure. We all have personal stories to tell, of things that we thought were failures only to become stepping stones to success.

The lucky few are a tiny minority who got the blessing of being written off as failures only to shame the writers with their bold narrative of resounding success.

It is a situation many sportspeople face. It is the same case with all kinds of competitive performers—be they actors, musicians, or others. There are low moments, and since competitive performers are well-known, these low moments get amplified. And as you know, negative news spreads much faster than positive news. It can dampen one's spirit, so many succumb to drug abuse and even suicide. But the hardened get fitter and finer. Be hardened, get fitter, and be finer. And that is the purpose of challenges.

Maybe, if we realized that pain and suffering is a norm of life, we would suffer less. Perhaps if we hugged pain and suffering without blaming, Karma would be worthwhile.

The common adage goes, "NO PAIN, NO GAIN." Is it true? Is it a fact of life?

Let's ask it differently; is there gain without pain?

And what is this "pain"?

Maybe, the best way to understand this common adage is to seek to understand the meaning of pain.

WHAT IS PAIN?

From a neuropsychological perspective, pain is simply an alarm. It is an alarm that alerts the body to an unpleasant, risky, and dangerous condition.

For example, when you touch fire, you feel pain, and it quickly alerts you to keep away. When you hurt your toe, pain alerts you of this condition so that you change your behavior, and also seek medical help.

Thus, pain is not a real occurrence but merely an alarm about it. For example, when a security alarm sounds off to warn against intrusion, the alarm is not the intruder. The alarm is not the thief, but simply an alert— a warning.

What you do about the alarm is up to you, not it. But, unless you switch it off, it will continue ringing for as long as the condition persists. It is why sometimes we take painkillers; to switch off our biological alarm, pain.

We do not heal that which the pain points us to but instead mute the sensations. Similarly, when you switch off an alarm, it does not necessarily mean that you have addressed the situation.

Can an intruder have access without an alarm sounding? Well, it depends on how the alarm is set up. Though rare, there are situations when an alarm fails to trigger, simply because the set parameters that help it detect the right conditions were not adequate. But, when it fails to trigger, that doesn't necessarily mean that the circumstances which it is supposed to alert you about have not arisen. You simply were unable to set it properly. And this setting is not just of the device itself.

First and foremost, this setting must first happen in the mind. The mind must be set, and it is this mindset that will activate the alarm. So, an alarm is simply a reflection of your state of mind.

With this perspective on the nature of pain, can you have gain without pain? Yes, it is possible, though rare. You gain happiness because loneliness warned you that you need friends to be happy. You become angry because conscience alerts you that you need to take action to remedy wrongdoing.

So, what is important is not about the pain sensations, but what these sensations are alerting you to. Life is full of painful moments, because, well, it is full of gains.

Whenever you experience pain, ask, "Where is the gain?" Search for it. Listen to what the pain is trying to communicate. Follow its cue.

Do not blame pain. It is merely a messenger of life.

IS SUFFERING INEVITABLE?

Buddha claimed that selfish desires cause suffering. Can a human genuinely exist absent of desires? Is there a difference between selfish desires and "non-selfish" desires? Do "non-selfish" desires exist?

Well, tough questions. As we ponder on these questions, let's ask ourselves, is there worthy suffering?

Maybe, before we can address this question, let's first of all digest what "selfish" means. So many times, we get confused by the semantics. What is the difference between "self" and "selfish"? Can you have a self without being selfish?

In the capitalist world, it is claimed that we are all driven by self-interests. Could there be a difference between "self-interest" and "selfish interest"? Let's assume so.

Inevitably we all have self-interests. I would argue that it is our self-interest that drives us to cater to others' self-interests.

On the other hand, it is our selfish interests that drive us to seek to deny others of their self-interests.

The pursuit of self-interest can bring peace. On the other hand, the pursuit of selfish interest can hardly achieve that. Selfish interests are more of a zero-sum game, Such that you can only gain by the sacrifice of another being. Such that you can only succeed through the failure of another. You can only live by the death of another.

In pursuing self-interest, there is potential for mutual gain. While, in pursuing a selfish interest, there is potential for mutual destruction. When you destroy someone else's self-interest, you may appear to experience momentary gain, but, eventually, you lose.

PAIN AND SUFFERING—WHAT IS THE DIFFERENCE?

We have seen that pain is an alarm. What about suffering?

Whenever there is suffering, there is pain. But, not all pain results in suffering. Why? Simply because suffering is a sensation, you attach to the loss that the alarm warns you about. If you do not feel a loss, then you do not experience suffering. You can feel pain without necessarily suffering, but you cannot suffer without feeling pain.

Suffering and pain have similar purposes, they are both alarms. Suffering is simply a state of continuous or persistent alert that you are losing something. It is like an alarm that stubbornly refuses to stop. In essence, suffering is a secondary alarm that alerts you to respond to the primary signal—pain.

Not until you address the cause of this pain, will you be worth it. To be worth your suffering is to understand its meaning. It is to understand the nature of suffering and respond to it in a curative way.

Like we said about pain, whenever you experience suffering, ask, "Where is this persistent gain?" Search for it. Listen to what the suffering is trying to communicate. Follow its cue.

Do not blame suffering. It is simply a messenger of life.

Buddha learned this. He followed his suffering to its ultimate gain—enlightenment. Had he chosen not to be worth his suffering, he would not have gained anything. He simply would not have achieved enlightenment.

A lot of times, it is in the most profound form of suffering that we gain the sharpest wisdom.

It is when you suffer to the near-death point that you realize the simplicity of life, you realize the facade of market success. You stop pursuing market glitters and do what is essential—just appreciating simple things like air, water, good food, and loving friends.

It is at the arrival at this point of discovering life's simplicity, and life's ultimate essence that you become worthy of your suffering. You become worthy of your pain because you are no longer wasting your life pursuing that which does not add value to it. You don't worry about the facade of success.

SIMPLE SUSIE

Susan Boyle rose to fame when she seemingly came out of nowhere to surprise millions of viewers with her otherworldly voice.

What made her stand out from the other contestants was her unassuming appearance. The judges did not think much of her at first, but when she sang "I Dreamed a Dream" from Les Miserables, it blew everyone away.

From then on, she became an international sensation. Susan became a household name and even got to perform with her idol Elaine Paige.

But it wasn't all sunshine and rainbows for Susan for most of her life. Born in 1961 in Scotland, she endured a lot of hardship and losses growing up.

Susan suffered some degree of brain damage when she was born due to a lack of oxygen while her mother gave birth. Although she started singing at the age of 12, she was often made fun of at her school.

Her classmates called her "Simple Susie" and other hurtful names. In spite of their cruelty, Susan did not let that stop her from taking part in her school's musical productions. After she left school, she kept singing as a hobby.

Susan eventually auditioned for a TV talent show in the mid-90s, but she got turned down. To make matters worse, her father passed away a couple of years after that. She then took care of her sick mother as her other siblings were married and had kids.

By 1999, Susan came out with a demo tape which she sent to radio and TV stations, hoping someone would recognize her talent. She even took professional singing lessons to improve her craft further. However, she enjoyed limited success—beyond her town of Blackburn, no one knew who she was.

To top it all off, Susan's sister passed away in 2000, and her mother in 2007.

With her chances of making it in the music scene dwindling and the loss of her loved ones hitting her hard, Susan found little motivation to pursue her dreams. With that, she put her singing career on hold, seemingly for good.

However, it was Susan's musical mentor that encouraged her to pick herself up and try again. In 2008, she auditioned for "Britain's Got Talent," which was her way to honor her mother.

And as she got up on stage, Susan was met with skepticism, laughter, and eye rolls. When she told the judges, she wanted to be as successful as Elaine Paige, they scoffed.

They could not believe that this ordinary, average-looking forty-something dared to take her shot at fame. The judges did not know what to make of her either—from the looks on their faces, they were not expecting much.

But that all changed when Susan started singing. They were flabbergasted that such a voice was coming out of the woman who stood before them. And by the time she was finished, everyone stood to give Susan thunderous applause.

CHANGING NARRATIVE

To experience success, we must change our narrative from that which confines us to limiting beliefs to that which exposes us to the world.

Susan Boyle's story is an example of how important it is to change your narrative.

All her life, people had labeled her and underestimated her. If Susan had believed the narrative that they forced on her, she would not have become the internationally known singer that she is now. She simply never gave a damn about their labels.

She refused to let negative beliefs tell her what she could or could not do. Above all, she believed in herself and what she was capable of. Even after decades of loss and heartbreak, she always held on to her beliefs, and that took Susan to places she could not have imagined.

Most people underestimate themselves and the power of their minds. When difficulties and obstacles arise, their natural response is to let these things affect their inner reality.

As a result, they allow these events to dictate their beliefs. When bad things happen, they take it as a sign that they are not good enough to deserve success and happiness.

However, those that successfully operate in the opposite direction do not let external circumstances affect them. Instead, they have an unshakeable core of grounded beliefs that influence the world instead of the other way around.

Throughout their lives, they have cultivated the mental habit of creating powerful beliefs that manifest into reality. It is as if their minds operate on a higher frequency, which sends out a message to the Universe.

What most people do not realize is that the quality of their thoughts is directly related to the kind of reality they manifest in their daily lives.

When they emotionally react to negative events or people, it starts a destructive cycle. The negative thoughts and beliefs in their minds attract more of the same.

When your beliefs center on hopelessness and misery, it affects your actions and sets the stage for even more negativity. But once you're aware that you're doing this in the first place, you can call yourself out.

For instance, when something wrong happens or when someone tells you something hurtful, do not let it poison your beliefs. You are not what happens to you, nor the labels people put on you.

You are what you think, and you become what you believe in. You do not need permission from anyone to be who you want to be.

Starting today, you have the power to create beliefs that will help you get to where you want to go. If you have struggled with trying to break free from your old beliefs, do not worry, I will show you how to supercharge your belief system so that you create the reality you want and live your dream life.

CHAPTER SIX

PASSIONATE PERSEVERANCE

One of the fascinating concepts of the Theory of Evolution as advanced by Charles Darwin is the concept of "SURVIVAL OF THE FITTEST".

The survival of the fittest is instead an apparent natural phenomenon. You only need to observe how animals behave in the wild to see it. However, that is still far off, a keen observation as to how humans behave can show you the traits of this phenomenon.

What Charles Darwin did was to increase the depth and width of understanding this phenomenon by shedding more light on it and making it not something to be assumed, but something worth keen attention and more in-depth focus.

In relationships, schooling, careers, etc., you will realize that those who achieve or surpass set standards are often the "fittest'."

In life, competition is the norm rather than an exception. Children learn early in life to compete for parental attention and love. This continues throughout their lives.

Even before conception, embryologists attest that sperms compete to reach the ova. The fittest, out of almost a billion sperms, is the one that succeeds in fertilizing the ovum. The rest are flashed out as having lost the game.

Observing competition deeply, you realize that it is instinctively based on hunting, a ferocious pursuit.

We often hear of job hunting, hunting for a mate, hunting for career opportunities, and hunting for prizes. A lot of times, it is those who cast shame aside that become shrewd hunters.

The gist of "HUNT WITH PASSION" is that, whatever we are hunting, we should pursue wholeheartedly. If we are hunting for "achievement," let's do it to the fullest. Let's not leave room for shame, pretense, and hypocrisy. Let's not be like "I want it but, I don't." This breeds confusion in our minds and yields frustration and suffering.

Other than occasionally being physically hurt while in hot pursuit of its prey, a hound never suffers the consequences of shame, pretense, and hypocrisy as humans do. Even being physically hurt in the normal course of pursuit does not necessarily yield suffering, except physical pain. There is simply no regret when you know that such is the potential cost of winning.

Hunt with passion. Don't listen to naysayers. Don't worry about shame—hunt with a stubborn determination.

Pain and suffering are an inevitable part of the hunting process. Every winner has experienced pain. Every winner has experienced suffering. To the winner's mind, there is great irony in pain and a great paradox in distress. It is the game of life.

INDOMITABLE WILL

Let the kicks of life not deter you. Harbor no excuses nor shame for your quest. Have an indomitable will to emerge victoriously at the end of the battle.

If there is one American president who epitomized both failure and adversity, it was Abraham Lincoln. Lincoln had numerous odds against him, odds that would make most people simply give up on their pursuits. However, Lincoln exemplified the sheer persistence and determination that is emblematic of the pursuit of the American dream.

Abraham Lincoln led the country during its most difficult moments. He kept the nation united amidst divisions. His determination, guided by his convictions, became the glue that bound the nation—right from his heart. Looking at Abraham Lincoln, you can feel the indomitable spirit that guided his mind.

Poverty is not a lifetime condition—unless you make it so. Adversity, like a battery, has both positives and negatives—which heightens your potential to achieve greatness. In this potential difference between the positives and negatives rests your charge for greatness.

You are not what happens to you. You are far greater than the sum of all events and circumstances that happen in your life. Don't identify with them. Rise above them!

Every adversity is an opportunity for greatness. If your adversity is mercilessly relentless, stop for a while and ask: "What treasure is it trying to alert me to that I cannot see?" There is always greatness in adversity. . . . it is up to you to define its form and occurrence.

In life, you will learn that those who threw the veil of shame away are the ones' that ended up revered by the very same society that insists on wearing this veil.

Let's look at the "small things" that we are already awoken to rather than these big things that the depth of our sleep cannot allow us out of, at least not for now.

"Small things!" What are they? Yes, matters of personal development, personal happiness, and personal success, among others. Yes, PERSONAL! Let us not go beyond that for now.

Society is complex, and peeling oneself from it may take us longer than the length of this book.

ELIZABETH ARDEN

What would cosmetics be without Elizabeth Arden?

While cosmetics are regarded as skin-deep, Elizabeth's beauty went beyond the boundaries of the skin. Her beauty was skull-deep.

Through her unique creativity, millions of women across the world could afford to mesmerize others with all kinds of skin shades and styles. The entrepreneurial spirit that oozed from Elizabeth's beautiful mind not only created sizeable wealth for her but also ushered in a multi-billion-dollar modern cosmetics industry.

Born Florence Nightingale Graham in 1884, to a farming family that struggled to meet its financial ends, Elizabeth wasn't deterred by either poverty or the farm life. She pursued her passion for beauty to a world far beyond the horizon of farmland plantations.

Elizabeth Arden trained as a nurse. However, she dropped out of nursing school to work in a pharmaceutical company as a bookkeeper. Her fascination with skincare meant she spent a lot of her free time in the lab there learning about skincare products. This gave her a familiarity with the scientific approach to doing things. There is no doubt that her training as a nurse helped her, for she probably wouldn't have gotten access to the labs if not for this.

She quickly employed her time in the labs to the formulation of skin care products, and eventually this ushered in a new world of make-up and other cosmetics.

The most important lesson we can learn from Elizabeth is that being born into poverty doesn't require you to remain poor. It doesn't define you. In order to change your circumstances, the most important factor is to spend your time acquiring all the skills you can that are necessary to advance your passion. Passion without skills is like faith without action. You've got to empower your passion with adequate skills, if indeed you desire to have your way.

The most important thing in turning your passion into a fortune is to have direction. Elizabeth had direction. She quickly quit her nursing course when she realized that it was not the direction of her passion.

She took on jobs that enabled her to explore more about her passion. For example, bookkeeping was odd, but knowing that it was in a pharmaceutical company where she could have access to labs, she took it up. Knowing that she needed practical skills in terms of applying her cosmetics to her clients and being able to demonstrate their potency, she took a job as a facial therapist.

With this blend of skills, Elizabeth became confident enough to launch her line of products—in ways that had never been known before.

At the time she was launching her products, the market had been saturated with the negative perception that make-up was only for women of low morals—especially prostitutes. She had to work hard to remove this negative perception from the market by changing the narrative. And with that change of narrative, she cleared the obstacles and attracted new clients. She had marvelous results, becoming one of the world's wealthiest women in her time.

So, do not shy away from developing an innovative product simply because the market has negative sentiments about similar products. It is your task to change the narrative and win over brand followers. Don't anticipate failure simply because others have failed. Do it differently, and you could find success where they couldn't. As Elizabeth advises, business is always there if you look for it.

HELEN KELLER

Have you ever imagined what your life would have been if you were blind? What if you were both deaf and blind?

Most of us cry out loud for the "misfortunes" that we face in life, yet, we have no permanent disability of any kind. Yet, one little girl by the name Helen Keller faced all three calamities that completely shutter one's ability to communicate in such a way that can be understood.

If you are told that Helen Keller not only wrote, but also spoke, and addressed multitudes with powerful speeches, you can hardly believe it. Yet, it is not that she was touched by a miracle that made her see, hear, or talk. . . but, by sheer determination, she learned how to turn her adversity into her greatest opportunity. She used her blindness to "see," and her deafness to "hear,". It is not that there were changes in these physical conditions. No. She learned how to rise above these physical limitations.

Her book The Story of My Life continues to inspire many. . . most of them people who have already lost hope in life, not because they are disabled, or face misfortune, but because she made them see the obstacles that they face as stepping stones to climb higher.

Helen Keller, like many disabled people who have gone the extra mile, has proved to the world that disability is not inability. However, it is easier said than done. Nevertheless, just as they proved, there is nothing that can't be achieved with effort and determination. To such disabled people, it is more than just effort, it is extra-ordinary effort; and not just determination, but persistent determination.

Having the sheer willpower to go against all odds is what counts, not your birth condition, not your family background, not your existing circumstances, and not your physical status. This is what Helen Keller's story demonstrates to us.

Your eyes can see, your ears can hear, and your mouth can talk. Why do you feel miserable? Make Helen Keller's achievement be the lowest possible challenge for you today. Dare to achieve more. Your destiny is in your mind, and that which you are seeking out there can only be found in you. The outside world is just a reflection, or rather, a shadow of that which is within.

Achievers are those who were dumb enough not to know that their pursuits were impossible; those who see "impossibility" and surrender get lost in the mass of mediocre averages.

The only thing worse than being blind is having sight but no vision. As Helen proves to us, it is better to have vision without sight than sight without vision.

BETHANY HAMILTON

What do you think would happen to you if you lost your arm to a shark at the tender age of thirteen? Would you go back to the sea knowing very well that sharks reside there?

Well, most of us would develop a strong phobia against water bodies, especially seas and oceans, which sharks call their home. However, Bethany Hamilton did what many would recoil from in their imaginations.

After losing her left arm to a shark attack and almost losing her life altogether, she recovered and within months went back to pursue her beloved passion—surfing.

Surfing with one arm? Yes, it can be less difficult if you were born with one arm, but when you lose it later in life, learning how to use only one arm to pursue such an extreme sport is quite a daring adventure. More daring is the fact that you are going back to the same risky environment where you lost your arm in the first place.

Yet, the loss of her arm never dissuaded Hamilton from pursuing her dream—to be a professional surfer. With just one arm, Bethany has participated in many surfing competitions and won many titles.

What would have ended her passion drove her to pursue it with greater zeal. She is not only a successful surfer but also a global inspiration to many. She used her lost arm to open doors to greater opportunities. She used her lost arm to write an epic autobiography Soul Surfer: A True Story of Faith, Family, and Fighting to Get Back on the Board.

She has accomplished much more with one arm than she probably would have accomplished with both arms. She turned adversity into opportunity. She did not allow adversity to mark her as a failure. She was undeterred, uncompromising, and unyielding in her resolve to pursue her passion and achieve her dreams.

Thus, do not cry because you have less. Be happy that you even have that less. Sometimes less is more. So many people are greatly endowed but end up miserable and mediocre because they did not appreciate what they have. They simply compare what they have with that which they perceive as plenty from others and feel miserable. Poverty is, in essence, a disease of comparison. Nature has already endowed you with so much that there is simply no reason not to succeed. Like Bethany Hamilton, seek out that passion; create that niche; marshal that force; with all these approaches, nothing will stop you from achieving your dream.

Many fully able people have buried their dreams based on a very flimsy dose of adversity. Like those who end their journey because a black cat crossed their path, many people are wrecked from their failed dreams. They gave up. They searched for excuses to give up— and got them in plenty.

Bethany proves to us that, with sheer determination and persistence, adversity becomes not an obstacle but a facilitator of your dream. Take a second look at what you consider as your obstacle and ask yourself "how can I get the hidden opportunities in this?" Every obstacle is a hidden bundle of opportunities. Every adversity is a hidden bundle of blessings. Opportunities and blessings happen to those who dare overcome obstacles and crack the hidden code in adversity. You are blessed with boundless opportunities. Crack the code!

GEORGIA O'KEEFFE

To be a great painter without a great spirit is almost like painting in darkness. There is no greatness in a spirit if it is not free to boundlessly flow.

Georgia O'Keeffe is a famous painter known for her great artwork. Georgia's life was rich in spirit. Her spirit transcended her art form. There is a great deal to learn from her arts. But, the greatest lesson rests in the source from which her creativity was channeled into the brush. . . . her unique mind.

Georgia was unconventional. She was outside the ideal conformities. That doesn't mean that she went beyond the bounds of decency. No. Nothing extraordinary in that regard. What is extra-ordinary is her perception of life.

What brewed within her mind was simply transcendental. And she was fearless in her articulation of ideas. There was a rare gem of bravery that very few dare to possess. She wasn't shy of entertaining controversies, contradictions, ironies, and paradoxes. A casual consideration of some of her ideas would easily look ridiculous to shallow minds, but to the deep minds like hers, the depth of their meaning was simply unfathomable.

She created great paintings. But, her greatest paintings were the mental imagery that she cast across the thought domain. Other than painting, she wrote passionately.

Passion defined Georgia's work, thoughts, and expressions. This is the greatest lesson that she endowed her fellow mortal souls.

Be passionate in your thoughts, words, and deeds. You owe no one an apology for the expression of your passion. Don't withhold your words and deeds for the sake of limiting yourself to the imposed habits of "success" and "happiness." These two come and go. They are momentary states, and for a very important purpose—to keep you in constant change. If success and happiness were a permanent state, you would want to remain trapped there, and you would inevitably decay. Just as night disappears with its sweet dreams to pave the way to daily efforts, so does happiness.

According to Georgia, the days you work are the best. Immersing yourself in work, not as a drudge, and not because of the paycheck, but out of interest and passion is what makes the best moments.

Georgia considered it foolish to pursue a permanent state of happiness and success. She was a powerful proponent of constantly pursuing one's individuality. Not for selfish desires, but to achieve your vision and the best in you. To her, someone else's vision would never be as good as one's own ambition. Thus, in as much as you may be awed by someone's success, let it be an inspiration to create and pursue your own work. Let it not be the darkness that steals light from your vision. In her perspective, if you haven't lived your dream, then you haven't lived any vision at all.

From this perspective of pursuing your individuality, Georgia advises that you should let criticism and flattery flow just as you let a river flow endlessly unperturbed. Inevitably, there will be flattery and there will be criticism from people around you. It is neither your fault nor within your control. Like a river, just let it flow. . . . if necessary, draw the little you can—for the sole purpose of quenching your thirst in the pursuit of your vision.

And like most great minds, Georgia wasn't scared of solitude. She loved being alone most of the time. It doesn't mean that she never felt lonely. Like everyone else, she did. But, she wasn't scared of it. She knew that it is the cost she had to pay for the gains of solitude. Everything has a cost. What is important is to understand how much you've got to pay and be ready for it.

EMILY DICKINSON

Better known after her death than during her lifetime, the poet Emily Dickinson was a master of her craft.

Despite being extremely introverted and deliberately choosing a life of solitude, she never left her mind unoccupied. She spoke her mind through her poetry and people were able to read it and understand her long after she had physically exited this world.

During her time, her poetry didn't seem that inspiring. This is because her writing style was unconventional, and probably inspired more scorn and criticism than appreciation. But, several decades later, the world began to unravel from the artistic limitations of poetry grammar to embrace her unique style.

Emily Dickinson was ahead of her time. She was alone, but not lonely, for her mind kept her company, and she befriended many who became awed by her unique creativity.

Yet, Emily never desired that her work be published. It was a private collection. It was a secret gem. Like most introverts, she seems to have felt that publicity would erode its worth.

Being endowed with talent, yet not pursuing fame is what we can learn from Emily Dickinson. This does not mean that we can't seek money for our creative works. No, it simply means that we must not let the market decide for us whether we should pursue our passion or not. Unfortunately, there are millions of people who have let their passions go to waste simply because the market hasn't discovered their worth. If Emily had thought this way, she wouldn't have pursued her poetry. Today, we wouldn't be engrossed in the marvelous beauty of her words. She did it for the love of her passion. Let us do what we love and are passionate about, for it is what makes us come alive and fully live. In her poetry, she fully lived. And in her poetry, she still comes alive, even today.

We can also learn from her that being alone does not necessarily mean being lonely. Solitude can be greatly rewarding. . . . and to mine the inner wealth, solitude is the most important state. Too much noise in the pursuit of fame is like too much disturbance in a pond—you never get to fetch that purity of crystal-clear water.

Take time. Dig deeper into your inner world. Embrace your solitude. But, do not forget to note your discoveries. It could be what the world needs to transform from the stale stagnant pond of the status quo to the flowing river of freshness. Emily did it, through poetry. You can do it in your unique way.

CHAPTER SEVEN

OBSTACLES INTO OPPORTUNITIES

L ook out for obstacles, be a challenge-seeker. Opportunities will make you their master, and when problems become your prey, you become the most successful hunter.

One of the primary purposes of life is to look for challenges and solve them. Happy are those who have learned this simple secret.

Those who avoid challenges never have solutions. A solution is the most important weapon that you can equip yourself with.

Find challenges that test your limits. Successful people are in love with the process of solving problems and opening doors to new opportunities.

You might be thinking, "Why would anyone invite problems into their life? Shouldn't we avoid them?"

Well, it is not about looking for trouble or creating unnecessary drama in your life. It is something else entirely.

What I am talking about is choosing a meaningful challenge to take on—and getting a sense of fulfillment from it.

Unfortunately, many people avoid challenges and thus fail to get solutions. When they fail to get solutions, they become defensive when they are suddenly attacked by the very same issues that they sought to avoid.

Life is a blockchain of solutions. You were born because some people provided solutions that brought forth your existence. Your DNA is a blueprint of solutions to known problems. Problems that your ancestors solved. There are already a lot of answers in your mind.

All you need is to identify the problems that match those solutions. Your ancestors did not know the kinds of problems you would face, but they provided all possible solutions based on their experiences. Thus, it is up to you to find out the solution based on your unique problem.

Those who avoid solving problems, simply avoid discovering their being, and thus avoid success. You cannot be successful if you have not lived fully. Yet, you cannot live fully if you have not discovered your being. And you cannot discover your being if you have no problems to solve.

Find challenges to solve. Improve the already existing solutions so that you will be able to bequeath future generations with a better repository of solutions—some embedded in their genetic code. Know that your life is better because your ancestors sought out problems and discovered solutions. As you walk along the path of becoming an ancestor, make sure that you add a new pack of solutions to this repository.

Those who wait for challenges never solve them. But those who actively seek out problems end up finding their solutions.

Where there is Challenge, there is Opportunity. As we have seen before, a negative mind sees obstacles as problems, while a positive mind sees obstacles as opportunities. A barrier is simply anything that makes it harder to achieve your expectations.

Whenever there is a challenge, there is an immense opportunity. Every day, you face dozens of challenges, ranging from small to big. And by succumbing to inertia, we avoid many of them, thus letting unexploited opportunities fizzle out.

Challenges are hardeners. They are weaning agents. They strengthen your resolve. They make you prove a point. And the greatest joy is when you prove naysayers wrong.

GROWTH-MINDED

You need to realize that no matter how talented you are, you cannot rely on talent alone when the going gets tough; you need a tough mind and indomitable will to overcome obstacles and succeed.

Those obstacles are there for a reason. They are meant to sharpen you into a better person.

So, when you encounter some setback on your journey to success, you need to look past the problem. Opportunity is on the other side of that coin.

Yes, some situations can be frustrating, and you cannot help but feel demoralized at the moment.

But here's the thing: you can still force the rational part of your brain to look at the positive side of a problem. It will be hard to see things this way, but you have to try. And in time, you can train your brain to develop this kind of perspective.

The trick is to make a conscious decision to set aside those emotions for now and ask yourself; how can I capitalize on this problem? What did I get out of the experience? How will this help me grow as a person? What lessons did I learn?

So, if that obstacle you're struggling with is helping you GROW in some way, then you're on the path to becoming a better person.

Negative feelings like anger or helplessness will come to pass. It is crucial that you develop the habit of treating challenges as a stepping stone to growth and NOT as an excuse to feel sorry for yourself—or blame the world.

The last thing you want to do is be a victim of "The Tyranny of Now." This happens when you are so consumed by a problem occurring in the present that you cannot do anything other than feel bad about it.

Growth-Minded people love tackling problems. They enjoy learning from the experience and getting better at their craft. And once they are done with a challenge, they'll seek out the next one. It is a never-ending mission that gives their lives meaning.

For example, athletes and sports teams do this all the time. They show up to practice every day, they put in the effort, they train as if it is the only thing that their lives depend on. And they push past pain and exhaustion.

They come up with a game plan and try it out on the playing field. And when the other team beats them, they learn from the experience and change their strategy. Then they get back up and keep pushing until they win the championships. And after they are done celebrating, they'll start getting ready for the next season and do it all over again.

Be honest with yourself and write them down even if acknowledging these challenges, stress you out or make you feel bad.

I want you to get used to separating your emotions from the situation and start looking at them constructively.

More importantly, I want you to start looking at these things as opportunities for growth. So, go ahead and get these challenges out in the open and make it your mission to get overcome them.

Swallow your pride. Of course, you are going to slip up at some point, but that is part of the process.

And when that happens, someone might share their opinion or feedback about it. It could be a friend, family member, or a person you work with.

There once was a group of tiny frogs who arranged a running competition. The goal was to reach the top of a very high tower. A big crowd had gathered around the tower to see the race and cheer on the contestants.

The race began. . . .

Honestly, no one in the crowd really believed that the tiny frogs would reach the top of the tower. You heard statements such as:

"Oh, WAY too difficult!!"

"They will NEVER make it to the top."

"Not a chance that they will succeed. The tower is too high!"

The tiny frogs began collapsing. One by one ... Except for those who in a fresh tempo were climbing higher and higher.

The crowd continued to yell

"It is too difficult!!! No one will make it!"

More tiny frogs got tired and gave up. But ONE frog continued higher and higher and higher. This one wouldn't give up!

In the end, everyone else had given up climbing the tower. Except for the one tiny frog who, after a big effort, was the only one who reached the top!

THEN all of the other tiny frogs naturally wanted to know how this one frog managed to do it?

A contestant asked the tiny frog how the one who succeeded had found the strength to reach the goal?

It turned out . . .

That the winner was deaf.

Some criticism can be genuinely well-meaning and constructive, which might be a little hard to hear at first. But if you can put aside your ego for a second and listen to what they have to say, their feedback will help you improve your craft.

However, you will also get your share of naysayers. They have nothing helpful to offer and will try to put you and your work down for the sake of it. Their criticism is not meant to help you grow in any way, but simply to discourage you.

Do not let those people take the wind out of your sails. Their opinions are not a reflection of the truth, but a vicious and spiteful attitude.

Therefore, you need to filter out and focus on the kind of criticism that you can build on and thrive.

IF THEY DON'T MOVE, WALK THROUGH THEM

Kevin Hart, a stand-up comedian, actor, entertainer, and author, had to go through a ton of rejection and painful criticism before he made it big.

When Kevin was still a young, up-and-coming comic, he got turned down while auditioning for one of New York's most famous comedy clubs.

A lot of huge stars like Eddie Murphy started at the same club, and the exposure they got from it launched their careers. So obviously, Kevin had a lot riding on making the cut and getting his foot in the door.

However, after the audition, the club owner took him aside and told him point-blank:

"I don't think this is for you. I do not think comedy is your thing. You should find a job and look to do something else with your life because this isn't it for you."

At first, Kevin thought the owner was kidding, but then he said after that:

"Thank you for coming, but unfortunately, you won't be performing here—that's it."

It was a swift kick to the gut for Kevin, and it felt like he had the wind knocked out of him.

He was discouraged and thought about quitting, but then a friend of Kevin said:

"Why do you care about someone else's opinion? You are in charge of your destiny. You are in a competition with yourself. The day you give up on you is the day you give up on your dreams. If you are in the business of giving up on your dreams, then I do not want to be in the business of being your friend. I think you're talented, so why don't you stay true to what YOU think you can do."

Therefore, you need to push past those hurtful words and keep pushing toward your goals in spite of how you feel at the moment.

Over time, you will grow a thick skin against less-than-flattering criticism. And in the process, you'll LEARN something from it and get better at what you do.

Do not rely on your talent, but try to grow it. It may be nice when someone praises you for being talented or intelligent. But in the greater scheme of things, it's not helpful.

People who often get complimented like this tend to do poorly when they encounter a challenging situation. They are not willing to make the EFFORT to push the limits of their natural abilities.

Fixed Mindset people just want to stay inside that comfortable bubble where they do not have to challenge themselves.

As long as they do not have to do anything too hard, then they can keep believing they're smart and talented.

On the other hand, a Growth-Minded person does not mind breaking out of this bubble, even if it means doing BADLY at first.

They are more than happy to fall flat on their face, pick themselves up, and keep trying. It is a small price to pay for taking their talent to the NEXT LEVEL.

Therefore, you need to understand that being talented is not a golden ticket to success—it's only the beginning.

You need to take your natural gifts and refine it with good, old-fashioned effort. It is the only way to make REAL progress in your life.

Learn from other people's successes and celebrate them. Fixed-Minded people resent other people's success and feel threatened by it. Growth-Minded people, on the other hand, celebrate their victories and feel genuinely happy for them. Not only that, but they also draw inspiration from other people's success.

When someone else is getting their piece of the pie, Growth-Minded people are not worried it is going to make theirs smaller. They know there is plenty of abundance and prosperity to go around, so other people's success is also their success, too.

One of the best ways to grow is by drawing inspiration from success stories and learning from them.

Remember: there is a LESSON that goes with every struggle they have overcome. You just need to develop the humility and open-mindedness to see it.

NEVER MIND THE ODDS

In Kentucky, there once lived an older man, always as broke as a squirrel, living in a tiny cabin and occasionally driving a beat-up car. The only source of his income was a $99 social security check—a reward for the toil of his entire life. At 65 years of age, with bills skyrocketing and the old car no longer willing to keep carrying him, he decided that his miserable life was no longer viable.

At 65, old and frail, there was hardly any employment suitable for him. He thought about how he could earn a better living, and the only thing that came to mind was his secret chicken recipe.

Can a chicken recipe transform a life? He just did not have anything else to offer. But he knew it was a great recipe. His friends loved it and would lick their fingers dry while devouring it.

Equipped with this chicken recipe, the older man left Kentucky to try his luck elsewhere. A change of living required a change of residence, so he thought. He traveled far and wide, knocking on hotel doors, offering his mouthwatering recipe.

He even sweetened the deal by not asking for any payment upfront but simply offering the recipe for free, with just a small commission on the sales.

To the surprise of the older man, all he received was a bold NO that continued with over 1000 restaurants. Dejected, but not giving up, the older man persisted. He knew what he had was a culinary goldmine.

After 1009 rejections, the older man got one YES! And it is this one YES, which ushered in the multinational food franchise by the name Kentucky Fried Chicken (KFC). And with this one YES, Colonel Hartland Sanders not only changed his fortunes but also transformed the way Americans eat chicken.

Had Colonel Sanders given up on the 999th rejection, he would have died an unknown poor man with his chicken recipes. America and the rest of the world would not have experienced, not only the great chicken from KFC but also the sheer number of employment opportunities that KFC offered to the world.

The persistently stubborn determination of one older man transformed the way we understand chicken cuisine.

Just imagine how many people give up even before the 10th rejection? I have given up countless times. And when I reflect on those times I gave up, I realize that I gave up my power to impatience and a negative self-image.

Thanks to the stories of such people as Colonel Sanders and Thomas Edison, I have cultivated a stubborn determination to never take NO for an answer.

A 'NO' is just a junction wall that tells you to change direction. It is not a blockade. Keep persisting. Keep knocking on more doors of opportunity. Do not give up knocking for as long as there are other doors to knock on.

I hope you realize now that your attitude toward obstacles can either help you achieve your goals faster—or slow you down.

Obstacles in themselves aren't setbacks, but opportunities for growth. You always have the choice to do three things; keep at it and power through those obstacles, procrastinate and beat around the bush, or pack up and go home.

Going with the first option may not be the most attractive choice, but it is worth it. Try to enjoy the process of overcoming your challenges, and you will gradually develop a Growth Mindset.

IF YOU CANNOT FIND IT, MAKE IT!

Most of us know Jay-Z, that famous rapper. Jay-Z faced unsurmountable rejection from record companies as no single label was ready to sign him. Tired of this letdown, he simply decided to start his own company. Through his Record company, he was able to strike a distribution deal with Priority, that enabled him to make his Reasonable Doubt album which would eventually earn a platinum.

Unlike Jay-Z, many of us give up on our dreams simply because we cannot find what we are looking for soon enough. Failing to find what he was looking for did not dampen Jay-Z's spirit. Instead, it encouraged him to create for himself that which he could not find—a Record Company.

So, stop whining that you cannot find what you want. Stop scapegoating the lack of what you want. Stop blaming others for not availing it. Simply fold your sleeves and make it!

As the old saying goes, "NECESSITY IS THE MOTHER OF INVENTION."

Seize the moment and create what you cannot find.

Inventors are those people who stopped whining and started creating.

Do not throw away this rare opportunity to become an inventor.

It is only those who see LACK AS LUCK who transform their lives and the world.

OPEN UP

Like a petal, everyone has seeds of life. And everyone has an abundance of sweet nectar.

If the petal decided not to open up for fear of bees, pollination would not be possible. We would probably not witness the beauty of flowers. And the abundance of food available to us courtesy of pollination wouldn't be there.

Just like a petal opening up to allow the success of pollination to take place, so we should open up to allow the abundance within us to be exposed.

If a petal held the fatally limiting thought that its nectar is so valuable that it should not open up to the bees, it surely wouldn't achieve reproductive success. Yet, most of us humans wrap ourselves in our very own cocoons of inferiorities, thinking that sharing our inner worth with the world will make us lesser beings.

On the contrary, the more that we give to the world, the more we receive,, and the more we succeed.

The experience that we gain from exposure is the real success.

STOP BARKING

Stop Barking at Shadows and Obstacles. Kick the obstacles; if they won't move, climb on them, if this is not possible, go around them, if that is not possible, rise above them.

In ancient times, a King had a boulder placed on a roadway. He then hid and watched to see if anyone would move the boulder out of the way. Some of the king's wealthiest merchants and courtiers came by and simply walked around it.

Many people loudly blamed the King for not keeping the roads clear, but none of them did anything about getting the stone out of the way.

A peasant then came along carrying a load of vegetables. Upon approaching the boulder, the peasant laid down his burden and tried to push the stone out of the road. After much pushing and straining, he finally succeeded.

After the peasant went back to pick up his vegetables, he noticed a purse lying in the road where the boulder had been.

The purse contained many gold coins and a note from the King explaining that the gold was for the person who removed the boulder from the roadway.

There is no doubt that in life there are plenty of obstacles. The closest obstacle being inertia. More often than not, we see the magnitude of an external obstacle based on the magnitude of our inertia. As such, the external obstacle becomes nothing other than the shadow of our very own inertia.

Once you can overcome inertia, you are then able to overcome obstacles. It requires greater willpower to overcome your inertia than the force you need to deal with its shadow—the external obstacle.

Like a car traveling over a hill, it is the driving force within that matters. With willpower and sheer determination, you can clear most of the obstacles in your life.

GIFT OF REJECTION

One of the worthiest gifts anyone can give you is rejection. It is more likely for someone to reject you if they are being honest or truthful about their feelings. But it is so easy for someone to accept you when they aren't forthright about their reaction.

The truth hurts, and the reality of rejection cuts deeper. Yet, like a surgeon's scalpel, it is the thing that gets rid of that unwanted matter. It can ultimately diminish your problem.

JOSEPH

Joseph had a very disturbing dream. He confided in his brothers about it, but little did he know what his beloved brothers would do.

Joseph was sold by them, to the Egyptians, as a slave.

When questioned by their parents, they concocted a lie that wild animals had killed him. They even came with "his" bloodstained clothes as evidence.

However, Joseph prospered in Egypt. The Egyptian monarchy loved him. He was promoted and rose to one of the highest ranks, being put in charge of the Egyptian granaries since he had advised the pharaoh of a wise strategy to save grain from each harvest.

This was significant given the frequent and persistent droughts in that region.

Driven out from their ancestral home by pangs of hunger, his brothers came with their elderly parents together with many other people from their community who were strong enough to endure the biting hunger on their journey to Egypt.

In Egypt, they received all they wanted. They were treated in a special way. Unbeknownst to them, the Egyptian who took care of them was none other than Joseph, their very own brother that they had sold.

Joseph revealed himself during the last hours when they were about to return. Tears of joy from his parents were mingled with tears of shame and regret from his brothers.

While Joseph's brothers thought that they were extinguishing his dream, little did they know that they were participating in making it happen.

What would have happened to Joseph had they not rejected him? Probably, he would have succumbed to the vagaries of starvation.

It is the rejection that embraced him. It is the rejection that crowned him. It is the rejection that made him loveable and successful. It is the rejection that made him take care of his brothers and parents, and thus restored their battered dignity in their most severe hour of need. Joseph transformed the rejection and subsequent hardship he experienced into an opportunity.

CHAPTER EIGHT

STRIP NAKED

Nakedness is one of the essential gifts nature could give to anyone. To be naked and not ashamed of it is the strongest manifestation of bravery.

In nakedness, there is nothing left to hide. There is nothing left to cling to if the experience is fully experienced, and lessons fully learned.

Those who fear being naked can never have a child. It is in daring nakedness that we are able to procreate. Without this adventure, procreation would not happen in its natural way. It is from our parent's naked venture that we were born. And it is by the very same naked venture that we beget our children.

Our ancestors had very little clothing. At some stage, they had no clothing at all. They were just like Adam and Eve. Yet, that did not change their humanness an inch. Our nakedness does not make us less human—it is our guilty conscience that does. This guilty conscience is a product of our mind being conditioned over time. Uncondition your mind, and this guilt will disappear.

A baby never cares about nakedness. A baby does not get shy about being naked. Nakedness does not stop a baby from smiling or crying, or seeking attention. The baby simply does what comes to mind, unashamed, innocent.

Can the same be said of adults? No! Why? Because, in our minds, our society taught us that it is shameful to be naked. And hence, a particular guilt association was ingrained in us about nakedness. Moreover, a certain set of consequences was imposed and accepted as the outcome of being naked.

Would the outcome be different if we were taught otherwise? It is worth pondering. Yet, there are those societies in remote parts of the world such as the Amazon forest, Congo basin, and Indian subcontinent where its members unashamedly walk naked. Why? Simply because the sense of guilt has not yet been inflicted upon them.

You, too, can be unashamedly naked. Just undress your guilty conscience. Your guilty conscience is the dress that you have to undress, and, if possible, throw away, never to replace.

Contemporary adults are beings that have been robbed of their naked innocence. In our contemporary society, an adult that walks naked will either be deemed mad or ill-intentioned. Why? Because innocent intentions have been robbed from such a person. The person is judged guilty by the mere act of being naked.

Why do adults fear nakedness except within the privacy of their homes? There is simply nothing that changes on your body, whether be it in public or within your bedroom. Thus, what makes it "odd" is the fear of intentions and the fear of interpretations.

The fear of intentions is on the part of those who watch your nakedness. And the fear of interpretation is what goes on in your mind about what others are thinking of your intentions, not really about your nakedness. Both fears are simply perceptional. They are created in the mind. Hence, the problem is not the nudity but the mindset—un-naked mindset.

Should you walk around naked? Should you stand naked in public?

Well, we are not in the dark ages. We think we are in the days of knowledge and enlightenment. These days, we are more concerned about what others think about us than what we feel about ourselves. Not bad!

Then, what is wrong? The bad thing is to extrapolate this nakedness beyond nudity. When we extrapolate it beyond nudity, we fear to undress our very own minds. We hide from specific thoughts because we fear how others will perceive them. We fear to ask naked questions and thus dress them in pleasantries, parables, proverbs, innuendos, and other such disguises.

The result is that we lose our innocence. Moreover, we can't cry when we feel pain. We can't laugh when we feel joy. We simply mute our feelings and only express them to those whom we allow into the private closet of our minds.

However, history teaches us that those who achieved greatness are those who embraced naked minds. They stood out and nakedly explained what they stand for, unashamed.

The most surprising thing is that most people fear nakedly exposing their thoughts, but they are the ones who are ready to become followers of those who have dared to expose their naked thoughts.

The end of this all is that we become hypocrites. Aren't those movies with some form of nudity the ones that are the most watched? Aren't those songs with lots of sex content the ones that we love listening to? Aren't those catwalk models who are almost nude the ones that we admire most? Yes, these are what attract our attention and thus pull our wallets. Then, why do we get ashamed of what we are ready to pay a premium price for?

And so, what does it mean to be naked? To be naked is simply to be without disguises. It is to be in a state that is not dressed up by society's prejudices, judgments, perceptions, taboos, beliefs, traditions, and cultures. To be naked is to embrace oneself in one's nativity and innocence.

You cannot have an invincible mind if your mind is not naked. You have to undress it. You have to remove that garment that society clothed you in starting from the day you were born. A garment designed to appeal and appease society. A garment intended to create and cause uniformity among members of your society.

And with this societal garment, every member of society is worried about guilt, shame, and fear of going against norms, fear of not wearing the societal uniform.

If you desire to free yourself from society's mind traps, then you have got to be naked. Give back to society what belongs to it—its garment.

DARE

One of the many ways by which we hide our nakedness is by refusing to accept our mistakes and refusing to do things because we fear failure. Both mistakes and failures are forms of nakedness; they expose the ways we did not measure up to the clothing tailored for us by society. Yes, they show the torn parts of the garment clothed on us by society.

We fear the nakedness of making mistakes and failing to such a degree that we dress it with blame, scapegoating, escapism, lies, pretenses, and other kinds of fake garments. Worst of all, we fear the critics' fingers being pointed our way while we are naked. This terrifies us. And the thought of this terror constrains us into the societal garment woven for us while we were still babies, to such an extent that we refuse to grow up enough to tear it apart. As such, we remain dwarfed so that we may fit into this societal garment.

Do not fear critics. Critics are like spectators, and you are the player. If your play is influenced by what the spectators direct you to do, you will never play. It does not mean that you do not consider them, for they are an essential part of the game. But, you are the professional, and they are the amateurs, just as a doctor will listen to a patient, but the doctor will not act under the instructions of the patient. Similarly, listen to your critics so that you may perfect your performance, but do not agree to be under their guidance.

Society, by its very nature, is a mass of spectators. Listen to society, but do not accept being absolutely under its instructions. Those who have known this secret are the ones who have transformed societies, even though this process may have caused pain.

If you want to unleash your potential to its fullest, do not worry about your critics. Understand and appreciate their role, but do not forget that you have your role to play.

If you decide to join spectators, then the game ends, for you cease to be a player and they cease to be spectators, as they have nothing to spectate.

Play your role so that critics may have something to do, to point the finger at your nakedness.

To wake up every morning and face a new day with a bold and uplifted spirit is courage in itself. Many a day, one would simply wish to surrender to the comfort of inertia and simply not wake up. Still, courage pushes us to overcome this potential resistance and do what we can to earn our daily bread, and take care of others—be it as caregivers or taxpayers.

TEAR OFF SOCIETY'S GARMENT

Have you ever worn uncomfortably tight clothes while going to a martial arts session? Have you worn tight high-heeled shoes while jogging? Have you ever worn a school uniform during a wedding function? Or have you ever went swimming in a suit?

These are slightly uncomfortable experiences. Right for the wrong occasions. Yet, a societal garment is often a one-size-fits-all kind of garment.

It does not always fit your growth rate. It is like insisting that a seventeen years old person should wear the same clothes that she wore at age nine. Unhindered, you will continue to outgrow societal garments. So, to continue to fit into them, the only other thing you can do is simply become stunted and dwarfed.

To be stunted is to be less than what you ought to be. It is to limit your potential. It is to limit your opportunities. It is to constrain your energy bundle by not igniting it more, for then there is no capacity for expansion.

Thus, to be able to grow to your full potential, and unleash this potential to the maximum, there is no other way apart from tearing off the societal garment imposed upon you. It is by shedding this garment that you can expose yourself to the soothing breeze of opportunities.

Yeah, I have teased you about nakedness. We know that if you walk nude in public, you can be arrested and charged with an 'indecent act' or even ridiculously charged with "causing a public disturbance."

Well, I do not mean that you should start walking nude. The days of Eden are gone if they ever existed. I do not want you to choose whether to be Adam or Eve. No. I am interested in what goes on in your mind. Should this interest you? I confidently hold that it should, just as we found ourselves having been educated in a way that we did not deliberately choose.

It is time we start undressing our minds from the traditions, beliefs, attitudes, fears, and other undesirous bug-infested garments, so that we can regain our nakedness.

To say that your mind is dressed up is an understatement. Your mind is not only dressed up but also mummified. It is mummified by the garment of culture, traditions, beliefs, taboos, and fears. The garment is so tight!

Unwrap your mind. Let it be freshly naked. Let it be free from this garment of culture, customs, taboos, prejudices, and other such fabrics. Let it be nakedly free.

Step out of your cocoon. Experience life. Get battered. Suffer. Life is never free of pain.

A naked mind is an unashamed mind. It is a mind that is not indoctrinated. It is a mind that harbors no guilt. It is a mind that is free to experience adventure. It is a mind ready to explore its being. It is a mind that is not set up to fear failure. It is not a complacent mind. It is not a conformist mind. It is a mind that is entirely left to explore its very own nativity. A naked mind is a free mind.

KEEP YOUR MIND NAKED! Do not allow it to be influenced and dressed in other people's garments.

The only image that deserves to be in your mind is your self-image, not other people's perception of you. The moment you let other people sabotage your mind-frame with their image is the very moment you lose your self-image and all its beauty and vision.

Start disbelieving. Start doubting. Start questioning. Start turning everything upside down, and if you cannot turn it upside down, turn your knowledge about it upside down. Simply do not let your mind align with the known.

Let your mind find the unknown. Strip your mind of conventional learning. Expose it to the nakedness of exploration and discovery.

Start looking at the leeward side of things, not just the windward side. The windward side is that side from which events and happenings confront you. The leeward side is that side obstructed by these events and happenings. Climb over this mountain of obstruction to see what is on the other side, the leeward side.

You can start by peeping through the leeward side of being fired, of not being a master, of being dumped or dampened, of being pulled down, of being late, of being not so intelligent or overly intelligent! The horizon of this list is as endlessly invisible as the invisible wind.

THE LEEWARD COST

While we face the windward side in our dressed composure, there is the leeward side that rests undressed, yet obstructed by the massive curtain of our mind that is camouflaged as the mountain. We fear this leeward side—the unknown side of reality.

For so long as we have chosen the fear of adventuring to the leeward side, we have forfeited a profound opportunity. And this forfeited opportunity has a cost—the Opportunity cost.

In economics, the Opportunity cost is simply the cost of the next best alternative that has been sacrificed.

If you remain on the windward side without exploring the leeward side, then, you have to bear the Opportunity cost of being on the windward side.

Unfortunately, our fears make us bear this Opportunity cost. Yes, the fear of heights and the fear of falling. And above all, the fear of the unknown.

To make the hitherto impossible possible, you have to be too dumb not to know that what you are attempting is impossible.

Yes, the Wright brothers were too dumb not to know that it is impossible to fly above the ground. Early explorers such as Christopher Columbus and Vasco Da Gama were too dumb not to know that it was impossible for there to be new lands beyond the ocean.

All explorers and inventors were too dumb not to realize that what they were venturing into was impossible. And by their effort, what was hitherto unimaginable, became possible. Why? Because they were daring enough to expand their minds, yes, to undress the known so that they could expose their nakedness to the unknown.

If Thomas Edison had given up on his 900th experiment, he would not have achieved the hitherto impossibility—of a light bulb! And guess what? He would have been deemed as one of the dumbest people on earth. But, his persistent determination to climb over the obstructive mountain of impossibility across to the leeward side is what brought light to this dark leeward side.

Colonel Sanders never gave up on his recipes, despite the many NO's! that he received. Some considered his recipe a dumb recipe, but that never dampened his spirit; like a marathoner, he soldiered on, until he was able to surmount this huge mountain of NO! And thus he ushered in the leeward side of opportunities, the hitherto dark zone in the culinary world.

Many great stories abound of those DUMB fellows that dared cross to the leeward side. They did not shy away from bearing the Opportunity cost of impossibility.

Who are you to give up? Who are you not to be dumb?

Let no fear trap you on the windward side. Dare climb over the mountain of obstruction.

IF YOU ARE FIRED, FIRE UP!

Oprah Winfrey was born into poverty in rural Mississippi to a teenage single mother and later raised in inner-city Milwaukee.

Her mother, Lee, was having difficulty raising both Oprah and her sister, so Winfrey was temporarily sent to live with her father, Vernon, in Nashville, Tennessee. While Winfrey was in Nashville, Lee gave birth to a third daughter, Patricia, who was put up for adoption in the hopes of easing the financial straits that had led to Lee's being on welfare. Winfrey did not learn she had a second half-sister until 2010.

Winfrey's younger half-sister Patricia died of causes related to cocaine addiction.

By the time Winfrey moved back with her mother, Lee had also given birth to Winfrey's half-brother Jeffrey, who died of AIDS-related causes.

Winfrey has stated she was molested by her cousin, uncle, and a family friend, starting when she was nine years old, something she first announced on an episode of her TV show regarding sexual abuse. When Winfrey discussed the alleged abuse with family members at age twenty-four, they reportedly refused to believe her account.

At thirteen, after suffering what she described as years of abuse, Winfrey ran away from home. When she was fourteen, she became pregnant, but her son was born prematurely and he died shortly after birth. Winfrey later stated she felt betrayed by the family member who had sold the story of her son to the National Enquirer.

In high school, she said she was continually reminded of her poverty as she rode the bus to school with fellow African-Americans, some of whom were servants of her classmates' families. She began to rebel and steal money from her mother in an effort to keep up with her free-spending peers.

As a result, her mother sent her to live with Vernon in Nashville. Vernon was strict but encouraging and made her education a priority. Winfrey became an honors student, was voted Most Popular Girl, and joined her high school speech team at East Nashville High School, placing second in the nation in dramatic interpretation.

She won an oratory contest, which secured her a full scholarship to Tennessee State University, a historically black institution, where she studied communication. Her first job as a teenager was working at a local grocery store.

At the age of seventeen, Winfrey won the Miss Black Tennessee beauty pageant. She also attracted the attention of the local black radio station, WVOL, which hired her to do the news part-time. She worked there during her senior year of high school and in her first two years of college.

By 19, she was a co-anchor for the local evening news.

Winfrey was fired from her evening news reporter gig with Baltimore's WJZ-TV because she got too emotionally invested in her stories. A Baltimore TV producer reportedly told her she was "unfit for television news."

As a consolation, though, he offered her a role on a daytime TV show, People Are Talking.

The show became a hit, and Winfrey stayed for eight years. Winfrey eventually became the host of The Oprah Winfrey Show, which aired for twenty-five seasons.

By the mid-1990s, Winfrey had reinvented her show with a focus on literature, self-improvement, mindfulness, and spirituality. Though she was criticized for unleashing a confession culture, promoting controversial self-help ideas, and having an emotion-centered approach, she has also been praised for overcoming adversity to become a benefactor to others.

Winfrey also emerged as a political force in the 2008 presidential race, delivering about one million votes to

Barack Obama in the razor-close 2008 Democratic primary. In 2013, Winfrey was awarded the Presidential Medal of Freedom by President Obama and honorary doctorate degrees from Duke and Harvard. In 2008, she formed her own network, Oprah Winfrey Network (OWN).

Winfrey's career in media would not have surprised her grandmother, who once said that ever since Winfrey could talk, she was on stage. As a child, she played games interviewing her corncob doll and the crows on the fence of her family's property. Winfrey later acknowledged her grandmother's influence, saying it was Hattie Mae who had encouraged her to speak in public and "gave me a positive sense of myself."

TV columnist Howard Rosenberg said:

"She's a roundhouse, a full course meal, big, brassy, loud, aggressive, hyper, laughable, lovable, soulful, tender, low-down, earthy, and hungry. And she may know the way to Phil Donahue's jugular."

Newsday's Les Payne observed:

"Oprah Winfrey is sharper than Donahue, wittier, more genuine, and far better attuned to her audience, if not the world," and Martha Bayles of The Wall Street Journal wrote, "It's a relief to see a gab-monger with a fond but realistic assessment of her own cultural and religious roots."

Employment is the tightest garment, the one that most fear to tear apart and are hesitant to take off. One of the greatest fears of modern times is the loss of a paycheck. A paycheck means having a roof over your head, driving that posh car, going out and having fun, and paying all kinds of bills that you may incur here and there.

Our educational system is primarily oriented toward making us dependent on the paycheck. It focuses on making us better employees, better servants, and at worse, better slaves. Slaves? Well, is there freedom if you cannot do without a paycheck?

If your livelihood wholly depends on a paycheck, then that paycheck is money that you simply must get to live. Without it, you have no shelter; you have no food on the table; you have no fuel for the car; you have no money for many other things.

Thus, any opportunity to disrupt this vicious cycle of paycheck dependency is liberating. It is an opportunity to dethrone your master. Unfortunately, the fear that comes with that opportunity is terrifying. I do not advise that you become reckless, but it is important to cultivate that mindset that enables you to break this vicious cycle. Yes, so you can fire your boss!

I do not mean that everyone should be self-employed. Companies and the government need workers to operate.

Nonetheless, since workers are required, then it simply means some should go for a paycheck. If everyone becomes self-employed, then, those multinational corporations would not exist. Governments would not exist; imagine being without an army, without civil service, without presidents? Well, with a programmed mind, as scripted for us by the system, this would never be the case. However, there is a leeward side. Do not give up climbing the mountain.

Anyway, if you no longer enjoy your status of being employed, then there is no reason to remain stuck in employment. Sack your boss! However, if being employed is what brings you joy and happiness, then, be employed! We may all look similar in this labor market, but not all of us are cast from the same mold. Seek out your uniqueness. And gauge the Opportunity cost.

Yet, what I am against is not you being employed. What I am against is you being a paycheck slave—toiling like a drudge just to earn that paycheck, when your heart and mind tell you that you ought to break free from paycheck slavery.

AMAZON

A young boy was born in Albuquerque, New Mexico, to a teenage mother, Jacklyn Gise Jorgensen, and his biological father, Ted Jorgensen.

The Jorgensens were married less than a year. When the young boy was four years old, his mother remarried a Cuban immigrant named Mike.

This young boy eventually graduated summa cum laude from Princeton University with a degree in computer science and electrical engineering.

He had shown an early interest in how things work, turning his parents' garage into a laboratory and rigging electrical contraptions around his house as a child.

He moved to Miami with his family as a teenager, where he developed a love for computers and graduated valedictorian of his high school. It was during high school that he started his first business, the Dream Institute, an educational summer camp for fourth, fifth, and sixth graders.

After graduating from Princeton, he worked at several firms on Wall Street, including Fitel, Bankers Trust, and the investment firm D.E. Shaw. In 1990, he became D.E. Shaw's youngest vice president.

While his career in finance was extremely lucrative, he chose to make a risky move into the nascent world of e-commerce. He quit his job, moved to Seattle, and targeted the untapped potential of the Internet market by opening an online bookstore.

> "I was working at a financial firm in New York City with a bunch of very smart people, and I had a brilliant boss that I much admired. I went to my boss and told him I wanted to start a company selling books on the Internet. He took me on a long walk in Central Park, listened carefully to me, and finally said, 'That sounds like a really good idea, but it would be an even better idea for someone who didn't already have a good job."

He respected the advice but didn't take it.

> "That logic made some sense to me, and he convinced me to think about it for forty-eight hours before making a final decision. Seen in that light, it really was a difficult choice, but ultimately, I decided I had to give it a shot,"

Jeff Bezos opened Amazon.com, named after the meandering South American river, after asking 300 friends to beta test his site. In the months leading up to launch, a few employees began developing software with Bezos in his garage; they eventually expanded operations into a two-bedroom house equipped with three Sun Microstations.

The initial success of the company was meteoric. With no press promotion, Amazon.com sold books across the United States and in forty-five foreign countries within thirty days. In two months, sales reached $20,000 a week, growing faster than Bezos and his startup team had ever envisioned.

Amazon.com went public in 1997, leading many market analysts to question whether the company could hold its own when traditional retailers launched their own e-commerce sites. Two years later, the start-up not only kept up but also outpaced competitors, becoming an e-commerce leader.

Bezos continued to diversify Amazon's offerings with the sale of CDs and videos in 1998, and later clothes, electronics, toys, and more through major retail partnerships.

While many dot.coms of the early '90s went bust, Amazon flourished with yearly sales that jumped from $510,000 in 1995 to over $17 billion in 2011.

As of 2018, the company had surpassed 100 million paid subscribers for Amazon Prime.

Bezos said:

> "I didn't think I'd regret trying and failing. And I suspected I would always be haunted by the decision to not try at all. After much consideration, I took the less safe path to follow my passion, and I'm proud of that choice."
> "I think the great thing about humans in general is we're always improving things. And so, if entrepreneurs and inventors follow their curiosity and they follow their passions, they'll figure something out and they'll figure out how to make it,"
> "And they're never satisfied. You need to harness that."

Though pursuing a new or innovative idea will be hard, but it is absolutely important.

When it comes to being fired, for most employees, this is one of the most tormenting moments of their lives. It is one of the darkest hours of their lives. Being fired is like the proverbial sword of Damocles that hangs over every worker's head. It scares most of them into submission. A slight threat of it by the boss brings about a high level of submission.

Yet, very few succeed in keeping this sword from piercing through their skull to empty their brains. Most people either blame themselves hard or blame their employers for the fall of this sword that ravages more people than it saves.

However, the few that allowed this sword to pierce their skull and allowed great ideas to flow, are the ones who discovered the marvels of creativity that lay hidden within them. The change paved their way to great success. It opened up a red carpet for them to higher places than their jobs ever could.

Those who fail usually fail not because they are not qualified enough, but because they are not persistent enough. Not being qualified to join the University of Southern California didn't stop Steven Spielberg from persisting in his dreams. He still got that degree after three rejections. He still achieved his career dream despite the rejection and without that degree.

Although most of the successful individuals faced rejection at some point, they never stopped hunting because of an obstacle in their way. They did not give up simply because the prey was too far away or because they were too slow. They trusted their guts, had faith in their instincts, and employed their inner power toward their pursuits. They simply did not give a damn about the obstacles.

Stop Co-Creating Your Master. The best way to start being a master is to stop being a slave. To stop being a slave is to stop the fear narrative that you have used to create a master. Remember, it is slaves who create their master, and not the other way around.

A lot of employees always make their relationship with their employers into a one-sided master-servant relationship rather than a two-sided partnership.

You do not need your employer more than your employer needs you. You need each other equally, unless you become more desperate and tilt the balance against you.

What makes most employees tilt the balance against themselves is nothing but fear, fear of loss of the next paycheck. For so long as your employer gets that subtle signal that you are desperate, the employer becomes your master, and you become the slave. Not because the employer has made you a slave. . . . but because you have made the employer your master. I must emphasize that working for someone does not make you a slave. It is working against your will, instinct, and aspiration that does. If you are happily working for someone, you are not a slave, keep it up!

JOBS

Steve Jobs was born in San Francisco, California. He lived with his adoptive family in Mountain View, California, within the area that would later become known as Silicon Valley.

As a boy, Jobs and his father worked on electronics in the family garage. Paul showed his son how to take apart and reconstruct electronics, a hobby that instilled confidence, tenacity, and mechanical prowess in young Jobs.

While Jobs was always an intelligent and innovative thinker, his youth was riddled with frustrations over formal schooling. Jobs was a prankster in elementary school due to boredom, and his fourth-grade teacher needed to bribe him to study. Jobs tested so well, however, that administrators wanted to skip him ahead to high school—a proposal that his parents declined.

After high school, Jobs enrolled in Reed College in Portland, Oregon. Lacking direction, he dropped out of college after six months and spent the next eighteen months dropping in on creative classes at the school. Jobs later recounted how one course in calligraphy developed his love of typography.

Jobs took a position as a video game designer with Atari. Several months later he left the company to find spiritual enlightenment in India, traveling further and experimenting with psychedelic drugs.

Back when Jobs was enrolled in Homestead High School, he was introduced to his future partner and co-founder of Apple Computer, Wozniak, who was attending the University of California, Berkeley.

When Jobs was just twenty-one, he and Wozniak started Apple Computer in the Jobs' family garage. They funded their entrepreneurial venture by Jobs selling his Volkswagen bus and Wozniak selling his beloved scientific calculator. Jobs and Wozniak are credited with revolutionizing the computer industry with Apple by democratizing the technology and making machines smaller, cheaper, intuitive, and accessible to everyday consumers.

Jobs looked to marketing expert John Sculley of Pepsi-Cola to take over the role of CEO for Apple.

The next several products from Apple suffered significant design flaws, however, resulting in recalls and consumer disappointment. IBM suddenly surpassed Apple in sales, and Apple had to compete with an IBM/PC-dominated business world.

Then, Apple released the Macintosh, marketing the computer as a piece of a counterculture lifestyle: romantic, youthful, creative. But despite positive sales and performance superior to IBM's PCs, the Macintosh was still not IBM-compatible.

Sculley believed Jobs was hurting Apple, and the company's executives began to phase him out. Not actually having had an official title with the company he co-founded, Jobs was pushed into a more marginalized position and thus left Apple.

After leaving Apple, Jobs began a new hardware and software enterprise called NeXT, Inc. The company floundered in its attempts to sell its specialized operating system to mainstream America, and Apple eventually bought the company for $429 million.

In 1997, Jobs returned to his post as Apple's CEO. Just as Jobs instigated Apple's success in the 1970s, he is credited with revitalizing the company in the 1990s.

With a new management team, altered stock options, and a self-imposed annual salary of $1 a year, Jobs put Apple back on track. Jobs' ingenious products (like the iMac), effective branding campaigns, and stylish designs caught the attention of consumers once again.

In the ensuing years, Apple introduced such revolutionary products as the Macbook Air, iPod, and iPhone, all of which dictated the evolution of technology. Almost immediately after Apple released a new product, competitors scrambled to produce comparable technologies.

Being fired is not the end of the world. Many things can cause you to lose that job or be unable to carry it out. Why assume that you can keep it against all the odds?

The moment you remain stuck with an employer against your will is the very moment you lose an opportunity for the next job, even the opportunity to create your job!

I am not implying you should become reckless and lose a job without any foresight or planning. I simply mean that you should not let the fear of losing a job perpetually control you. Fear comes, and it is a good alert. However, when it manifests as nagging, it simply means that you are not acting upon it. Imagine if an alarm is alerting you of a robbery that is taking place, and because of your fear, you refuse to act. The theft will continue, and you will lose the opportunity to protect your valuables. The same can happen with a job.

The moment that fear of losing your job becomes profound, you have to start strategizing on how to fire your boss. Let your boss not be the one to pull the trigger, it is more joyful when you are doing it.

The confidence that comes with you pulling the trigger can fire you up to greater heights of inspiration. There is no bitterness; there is no blame; there is no scapegoating; you are accountable; it is your responsibility. It is the essence of being your own boss: accountable for your own well-being.

IF YOU ARE DAMPENED, GERMINATE!

In every being, there are plenty of seeds; the great ideas. Every being procreates these seeds every moment. Some seeds die because they are not nurtured, they are not encouraged to mature, or they are simply carelessly exposed for the "birds" to pick up.

We know the importance of moisture to seed germination. Yet, why do we abandon this important seed when dampened by those who do not understand their significance? Why would such a critical necessity for seed germination not to be seized upon?

When we fail to focus on this seed, the dampening moisture causes the seed to rot rather than to germinate. No matter how good the moisture is, without illumination and care, the seed can never germinate. Keep this in your mind! And do take it to heart!

It is common for water to be poured on your great ideas. There is hardly any person who made a great success out of their ideas that didn't experience cold water for being "crazy," "outrageous," "dumb," "a failure," etc.

There are more doomsayers in the world than those who brighten up the horizons. The most important thing is for you to let the light of your spirit illuminate your dampened seed, and let it germinate.

ANNA WINTOUR

The Vogue editor started her career in New York as a junior fashion editor at Harper's Bazaar. She made waves for her innovative shoots, and editor Tony Mazalla thought they were a little too edgy. She got fired after a mere nine months.

Getting fired was a great learning experience and never held back her style. "I recommend that you all get fired," she told fashion students.

Shortly after leaving Harper's, she became a fashion editor at Viva, and in 1988 she was named Editor-in-chief of Vogue, a job she has held for twenty-seven years.

Very few can stick to the same position for twenty-seven years and still excel. Wintour has been Vogue's editorial director for that long. Her creative prowess has enabled her to take over the more senior and challenging role of being the Creative Director of Conde Nast, an expansive mass media company with a global outreach. Conde Nast is the parent company to Vogue, the New Yorker, Glamour, and many other publications.

Anna Wintour exudes boldness, creativity, impactfulness, and above all, freedom. Without freedom of creativity, which allows one to explore, experiment, and come up with an ingenious product, she wouldn't have remained in such a hot position for that long. Being bold in her decisions and approach has ensured that Vogue carves out a brand that stands out against all seasons. While she is bold and decisive, she isn't aloof or inconsiderate. She has been able to build and support a strong team that she trusts to carry out the tasks that make Vogue remain steadfast.

Unlike some executives who ring-fence the secrets to their success, Anna Wintour has been ready to share her passion by being available to offer advice to those who approach her. Her seniority and heavy responsibilities haven't robbed her of the ability to foster other's talents. In addition, Anna Wintour still finds time to play the violin.

The success story of Vogue attests to the fact that Anna Wintour has been able to lead with impact. This impact has not only been felt at Vogue but across the entire fashion media industry and the wider leadership spectrum.

Anna teaches us the power of being decisive and consistent. With this power, you can mark and define your territory, and use the very same power to reign over it.

SHOUT OUT LOUDER

Edison was called dumb. His teacher apparently told him that he was "too stupid to learn anything." Like most stubborn people, he refused to give a damn about it.

Dumbness can be equated with being mentally "dark." Yet, thanks to Edison's invention, not only our homes but also our cities shine in the dark hours of the night. He ended up achieving a feat that shouted his naysayers down to a humble silence.

"You ain't goin' nowhere, son. You ought to go back to drivin' a truck."

This was the dampening rebuke that Elvis Presley received from his Record Manager, right after his first performance. He refused to give a damn about this negative assessment, and stubbornly pursued his passion.

History attests that Elvis Presley not only sold almost a billion albums but also had his name immortalized in the Rock and Roll Hall of Fame. He was the greatest musical icon of his time.

"Why don't you stop wasting people's time and go out and become a dishwasher or something?" is the dampening statement that Sidney Poitier received from the casting manager during his first casting audition. Had Poitier given a damn about this nasty question, he would not have made history as the first black actor to win an Oscar.

IF THEY GO LOW, GO HIGHER

This is an adaptation of Michelle Obama's famous quote, "when they go low, we go high" as a response to her racist critics.

When an eagle wrestles a snake, it knows that on the ground the snake is more powerful. But in the air, the snake becomes powerless. So, when the snake tries to wrestle out of the eagle's powerful jabs, the eagle soars higher, and the more the prey resists, the higher the eagle soars. Until it reaches a point where it can play games with the almost unconscious prey, leaving it to fall halfway and then seizing it back with its claws. After two to three times, the prey will be lifeless.

Similarly, when you are challenged to the ground by those who do not want you to rise, the best strategy is to rise, do those things that they are trying to stop you from doing.

And as Nelson Mandela said, "the moment you pin someone down, is the very moment you lose the power to rise." Do not lose your power to rise. Go higher, and as they try to fly beyond their reach in an attempt to harm you, they fall.

Most of those who never gave a damn about nasty remarks and insults about their inability to succeed eventually achieved their desired success. This includes Sidney Poiter, Elvis Presley, Oprah Winfrey, Steven Spielberg, and so many others. Their actions simply tell you, "Don't give a damn!"

It is the minds who suffer inferiority complexes that belittle others. This is because they try to cast their very own garment of limitation upon other people's minds. And if you accept this garment, your growth is stifled.

Invincible minds know that within each person rests infinite potential. Thus, they don't bother dressing up anyone's mind, but encourage each mind to expose its nakedness to the flowing currents of endless potential.

The invincible mind knows that, until the seed germinates and grows to a full tree, you will never know the sweetness of its fruits.

TOO LATE!??

It is never too late, until you call it late! Most entrepreneurs start early in their youth. It is considered the prime of creativity. When they're older, most people seek comfort zones for themselves and their families and thus shun the risky adventures of entrepreneurship.

However, Colonel Sanders was different—maybe not out of desire but out of compelling necessity.

Think about this other man.

At over eighty years of age, an older man wandered into the desert. This is the place he ran to avoid arrest after killing someone who had wronged him. The older man had lost hope of ever becoming any better in life. He had lost hope of ever reuniting with his community. However, a moment came when a voice of conscience challenged him to liberate his people from slavery.

He wrestled with the idea, resisting it so many times. He excused himself for being too old, for being a stammerer, for having committed such a heinous crime that his community would not accept his leadership.

He found every other excuse he could imagine, just to avoid leading his people out of captivity. Eventually, he lost the battle to his conscience.

History attests that this man not only overcame the self-inflicted fear that imprisoned him into self-exile but went back to his community.

He was not arrested. He was not rejected. But, amidst resistance from the slave masters, he launched the world's most renowned exodus of all time, emancipating an entire nation from captivity and leading them into the Promised Land. His name is Moses.

IQ IS OVERRATED. DO NOT BE DISTRACTED

When one mentions mind, intelligence lingers in its shadow. The mind is like a car, intelligence its engine. We may admire the car, but until we test the engine's capacity, we may not know the real power of the car. The same is the case with intelligence.

Gone are the days when IQ was the revered measure of intelligence. Gone are the days when academic performance in school was regarded as the absolute measure of one's intelligence.

Sorry to those who died falsely, thinking that they were dumb and unintelligent. Just as the earth was once considered to be flat and any other contrary notion banished, and just as Pluto was considered a planet and any contrary notion considered insane, those people considered slow simply weren't dumb.

Just as we have a multiverse, we also have multiple intelligences

The assertion that we only have eight planets in the universe no longer holds. The notion that we only have one universe also no longer holds. The new notion is that we do have a multiverse, each with its own set of planets. The sun is no longer the only known star to have planets revolving around it. Similarly, the solar system is no longer the only organized system of stars.

Just as we have come to the notion that we no longer have a universe but instead a multiverse, we have also come to the notion that we no longer have just one form of intelligence whose measure is the IQ. There are many forms of intelligence with different sets of measures such as the EQ (Emotional Quotient), SQ (Social Quotient), and even the ESQ (Emotional Social Quotient).

There is still debate about whether EQ and ES are independent of each other, or one is a subset of the other.

Astronomers and space scientists have not even concluded how many universes exist, let alone how many planets exist. It goes without saying that if you cannot deduce with absolute specificity the number of universes, then you cannot do the same about the number of planets. The discovery is still ongoing as we continue to refine our space exploration tools and redefine our standards of determination.

Similarly, we are still exploring different forms of intelligence and still establishing standards of determination of each form of intelligence. It would be stupid for anyone to call someone else dumb, lest it is only a matter of semantic expression of one's emotions.

Thus, like Einstein and Edison, do not give a damn when you are called "dumb." You simply are not. Just because you do not fit into someone else's shoes doesn't necessarily mean that you cannot fit into any shoe.

DO NOT JUDGE A FISH BY THE STANDARDS OF A BIRD

Judging from the foregoing, it is quite easy to conclude that IQ, as the intelligence measure we have all known, is overrated.

According to Einstein, we cannot judge a fish by the standard of a bird. Neither can we judge a bird by the standard of a fish.

If we judge a salmon by how intelligently it can fly in the sky, it will always be dumb. Yet if we judge a sparrow by how skillfully it can swim, then the sparrow will always be dumb.

Similarly, there are so many people we have condemned as dumb simply because they had a low IQ. Yet, they had some of the highest levels of ESQ.

Many people, such as Thomas Edison, Albert Einstein, and others, were considered dumb during their early stages of schooling. Nevertheless, they proved their judges wrong.

The best thing a formidable mind can do is not be trapped into these biased standards of measuring intelligence.

ARE YOU A MARATHONER OR A SPRINTER?

Whenever we participate in the Olympics, whether as spectators, coaches, or fans, we realize this is just a microcosmic representation of the nature of human endeavors.

Athletics is probably the best depiction of life's journey. When people compete in athletics, you can witness the sheer immensity of human power and determination.

Narrowing down athletics to only sprints and marathons, we can learn a lot about life. In running, these are the two extremes. There are many mid-races in-between. However, as in our bird and fish example, if you judge a marathoner by the standard of a sprinter, you will easily label the marathoner as clumsy, slow, and dumb and the sprinter as brilliant and dexterous. On the other hand, if you judge a sprinter by the standard of a marathoner, you will easily label the sprinter a lazy, low-energy failure.

Unfortunately, in a world where uniformity is the norm, identical standards are desired, and the average is the law, either you will be judged by the standard of a marathoner, or you will be judged by the standard of a sprinter, depending on what is considered the appropriate measure of success. Woe unto you if you are a middle-distance runner.

In the schooling system, a slow learner typically exemplifies a marathoner, while a fast learner typically exemplifies a sprinter. The average learner typically exemplifies a middle-distance runner.

Some of the most successful slow learners we have had include Albert Einstein and Thomas Edison. These two people were easily branded as dumb because they were too slow to grasp concepts in their formative years in school. Yet, history attests that they were some of the most intelligent brains that we ever had. They became great inventors and accomplished greater feats that those who branded them "dumb" could ever have dreamed of accomplishing by themselves. Both Einstein and Edison were marathoners and were judged dumb by using the standards of a sprinter.

Heaven forbids! What if Einstein and Edison had not lived to adulthood? They would have been permanently consigned to dumbness by their labelers.

The most unfortunate thing is that these labels were given by the very same people we entrust with the virtue of dispensing knowledge and education—parents and teachers.

The consolation is that EXPERIENCE IS THE BEST TEACHER. This is the ultimate teacher when everyone else fails in their duty and responsibility to educate society.

Unfortunately, there are many Einsteins and Edisons in our society who either never had an opportunity to prove their mettle, or simply paid too much attention to the labels that they were branded with and surrendered to the status they were given.

CHAPTER NINE

DEBUG YOUR SCRIPT

We are all thinking beings. There is very little that we can accomplish without thinking. The mind is the factory that manufactures thoughts. Reflection is a process, and its product is thought.

Like all factories, how the mind is designed determines what process takes place and what its eventual outcome is. What is important is to note that we are born with a very basic mind, packed with all we need to survive and adapt at the early stages. These include basic instincts such as sucking, swallowing, sleeping, waking up, and crying for attention. While there is a vast repository of genetic information stored in our mind, this gets activated over time as per our needs.

Apart from this inborn mind, the bulk of our mind is crafted through the learning process. Our parents become our first teachers, and the family becomes our first school. Later on, other teachers join in as the school expands beyond the household.

Most of what we learn from our parents is what their parents taught them. It goes back generations, and via ancestors, to time immemorial. In simple terms, we get imparted a set of beliefs, attitudes, and habits that form our cultures and traditions. This designs our mind in a certain way and alters our thought process. Eventually, our thought process yields a particular desired outcome.

More often than not, we tend to assume that the outcomes of our thoughts are unique. Yet, they are already set up by the learned mind. This is why most of us, given the same challenges or sets of data, arrive at nearly the same conclusions. There will be slight variations as there are slight variations in a manufactured product; however, there is more precision in a factory setting.

So, if our mind has been set up in a certain way to yield a specific desired outcome, why would we expect a different kind of outcome without changing this setup?

Like something that is beyond our full comprehension, it is not that easy to pin down the dimensions of the mind, let alone a formidable one.

We have already seen how the mind works like a factory. We have seen how thoughts are its products. We have also seen that outcomes are already anticipated. It is because the setup, like any factory, is designed to yield a particular outcome.

Thus, expecting a different outcome from the same setup is pretty weird.

We have seen that this setup is informed by thousands upon millions upon billions of experiences. These experiences started from time immemorial and will continue until time unknown, whether you procreate or not, and for so long as human species continue to exist.

When you see yourself, you are simply a dot in a long script that precedes it. Whether the line will continue after the dot depends on whether you will choose to prolong it to the next dot or not.

Your children are the new dots you create to prolong this script. The script's content represents the narrative of your experiences with your environment and relationships.

You have the power to rewrite your script. You can curate its content to bring forth the meaning that you desire. You are the writer, editor, and publisher of your mind's script. You are your mind's curator.

When we talk about the script, it is quite profound. More in-depth than just words. To the writer, the script is just a narrative. To the actor, the script has a drama. To the programmer, the script has codes that make it software. To the politician, the script has power. Moreover, to the prophet, the script has magic.

You can choose to be a narrator, you can choose to be an actor, and you can choose to be a programmer. You can also choose to be all these, plus more. It is all within your power.

The same can be said of your mind. Your mind is an infinitely complex web. Yet, we have a conscious mind, which is simply a distilled illusion of what underlies it—the subconscious and unconscious mind.

Knowing how to bend to the extreme, yet not break, is the art of the wise. The wise know that rules can be bent, and norms can be stretched, it all depends on the context and demands within it. Every law has exceptions, and every context has different perspectives. Blending an exception with an alternative perspective is the skill of the wise.

Giving too much power to worry and anxiety is unwise. It is a refusal to blend the exception with an alternative perspective. It could be as a result of not being keen enough to find the exceptions or not insightful enough to illuminate an alternative perspective; or it could be both. It could also be a fear of the outcome of this blending. Whichever the case, too much worrying is unwise.

If you cannot find an exception, create one. If you cannot find an alternative perspective, forge one. The experience you gain from this creativity will formulate your wisdom.

Masters are those who derive their power from that potent blend of the exceptions with alternatives. Masters are above the law, and the law is subject to them. Thanks to their wisdom.

Unfortunately, slaves fear exceptions and hate alternatives. They prefer being subjects on the conveyor belt of the master's mind factory.

LONGER THAN YOU CAN HOLD

Once upon a time, a psychology professor walked around on a stage while teaching stress management principles to an auditorium filled with students. As she raised a glass of water, everyone expected they would be asked the typical "glass half empty or glass half full" question. Instead, with a smile on her face, the professor asked, "How heavy is this glass of water I'm holding?"

Students shouted out answers ranging from eight ounces to a couple of pounds.

She replied, "From my perspective, the absolute weight of this glass doesn't matter. It all depends on how long I hold it. If I hold it for a minute or two, it is fairly light. If I hold it for an hour straight, its weight might make my arm ache a little. If I hold it for a day straight, my arm will likely cramp up and feel completely numb and paralyzed, forcing me to drop the glass to the floor. In each case, the weight of the glass doesn't change, but the longer I hold it, the heavier it feels to me."

As the class shook their heads in agreement, she continued, "your stresses and worries in life are very much like this glass of water. Think about them for a while, and nothing happens. Think about them a bit longer, and you begin to ache a little. Think about them all day long, and you will feel completely numb and paralyzed —incapable of doing anything else until you drop them."

More often than not, we hold onto things when we would have been better off having left them to their death. One such thing is a grudge. The more you hold onto a grudge, the more it stresses you.

Sometimes we do have hopes, dreams, and expectations. That is great. They are important. However, they also have relevance range. They have an expiration period. The wisdom is to know when to give up on what is no longer worth holding onto. While it is good to be persistent, and while it is good to be patient, these too have limits. They are not unlimited.

Sometimes, what is needed is just to change your perspective and angle of view. Why push a wall when you can go around it? If the wall is very strong and solid and you cannot develop more strength, then no matter how long you persist and no matter how patient you are, you simply will not be able to push it away. You have to find a different way of getting it out of your way, and better still, getting your way out of it.

UNDERSTANDING THE POWER OF SIMPLY BEING

The most significant human tragedy is self-denial. We are perpetually denying our state of merely being. We constantly struggle to acquire what other people have.

It can be witnessed by the destruction we cause to our bodies in a bid to be more handsome and more beautiful. Yes, to fit into that mirror of market success. We convert ourselves into commodities for the market mirror.

That which the market deems as "beautiful" is what we pursue. In this pursuit, we destroy our true essence from within in a bid to acquire the market essence of others.

Aren't some of us seeking to be beautiful dolls for the market?

We undergo plastic surgery so that our flesh may be less bumpy. We plant artificial hair at the risk of damaging our natural hair. We go for injections to inflate our bums just as we pump air to inflate balloons.

We go for steroids to inflate our muscles so that we achieve the kind of body that the market tells us is "ideal perfection."

Why do we yearn to be who we are not?

Why is it that the gurus of "success" and "happiness" advise us that "you have to fake it till you make it"?

There is no doubt that the world is full of wannabees.

Yes, there are so many zombified apes touting the brands and imaginary lifestyles of their masters; they attempt to fake their authenticity just to appear like their masters.

Is it so impossible to simply be who you are?

What is so problematic in simply being?

We see fake mustaches, fake eyebrows, fake hair, almost fake everything.

Why do so many humans search for imaginary solace in fakeness?

Are they running away from their real being?

What is it that they are running away from?

Self-awareness is the mind's sharpening tool. Become self-aware, and you won't give a damn about illusions. You will have less risk of being deceived and being fed distorted knowledge. Self-knowledge is rejuvenating, refreshing, and authentic. Self-knowledge is your most durable shield against self-limitation.

MADAM C. J. WALKER

Very few people born into slavery could see beyond the horizons that the master set up for them—the slave yard. Yet, history surprises us with lessons about the few who chose to peer beyond the horizons of confinement that their ancestors and generations before them had been subjugated to, after being ferried like logs across the Atlantic from their native lands of Africa.

Yet, one woman decided to raise her chin high and follow the rays of hope to the life of her dreams.

Walker was born Sarah Breedlove on December 23, 1867, on a cotton plantation near Delta, Louisiana. Her parents, Owen and Minerva, were enslaved and recently freed, and Sarah, who was their fifth child, was the first in her family to be free-born.

Minerva died in 1874 and Owen passed away the following year, both due to unknown causes, leaving Sarah an orphan at the age of seven. After her parents' passing, Sarah was sent to live with her sister, Louvinia, and her brother-in-law.

The three moved to Vicksburg, Mississippi, in 1877, where Sarah picked cotton and was likely employed doing household work, although no documentation exists verifying her employment at the time.

At age 14, to escape both her oppressive working environment and the frequent mistreatment she endured at the hands of her brother-in-law, Sarah married a man named Moses McWilliams. On June 6, 1885, Sarah gave birth to a daughter, A'Lelia. She became widowed two years later.

Born the daughter of a slave on a cotton plantation, Sarah Breedlove wasn't ready to be dulled by this environment. She had a strong sense of beauty that flourished despite her circumstances.

To escape from the sad memories of her environment, she moved from Louisiana to St. Louis where her brothers worked as barbers. This also granted her the opportunity to become a hairdresser—a good opportunity away from her job as a cotton-picking slave laborer.

After a while, she began to lose her hair. This was due to a severe dandruff infection—a condition that afflicted many black women. She started struggling to save her hair as this had been a highlight of her beauty. She experimented with various solutions. Eventually, she succeeded in finding one solution that not only arrested dandruff but also helped her hair grow.

The entrepreneurial spirit in her immediately saw a grand opportunity—to earn a living while helping fellow womenfolk facing similar problems. She named her newfound product "Madam C.J. Walker," which was the name of her new husband, whom she later divorced.

Blending her marketing acumen with an entrepreneurial spirit, she branded her two products "Madam C.J. Walker Hair Grower," and "Madam C.J. Walker Shampoo," names which reflected the challenges black women were facing.

She became the mirror of her solution—not only a living testimony but also a walking testimony of what her products could do. Her products became high in demand from those who witnessed her struggle with dandruff and hair loss. Word spread around. She reveled in spreading it more. An evangelist of her product's gospel, she knew that word-of-mouth had power.

She employed sales agents who helped her market her brand. Soon, she was constantly touring across the nation, marketing her brand, recruiting more sales agents, and motivating those already in the field.

With her network of sales agents, she pioneered the direct marketing system that many companies such as Avon have utilized to skyrocket their sales.

Thus, she became not only an inventor but also a pioneer of a novel marketing system. She became not just the first African American female millionaire but also America's first self-made female millionaire.

If there is any great lesson one can learn about Madam C.J. Walker it is that adversity is a fair dispenser—of both the bitter and sweet. Often, we focus on the taste that adversity serves us first—bitterness—and instantly judge it as unwanted. By this lazy conclusion and quick surrender, we lose the opportunity to get to the sweet side of the basket.

Don't give up. Don't surrender to adversity. Explore it. Turn it upside down. If need be, crush it to find out what rests hidden within it. Study every element that comprises it. You will surely not miss a fortune. When it comes to adversity, FORTUNE TURNS TO MIS-FORTUNE only when you fail to exhaustively explore its hidden nature.

UNLEARN

By the time everyone graduates, there is an abundance of knowledge pumped into one just to fit the various conveyor belts and stations of existence. Through time, some (not most) discover that they cannot fit into this jigsaw puzzle. They are simply out of shape with the frame of reality and out of sync with their soul's purpose.

We can witness symptoms of this disorientation in terms of unemployment, drug abuse, depression, and suicide.

The only thing one can do is to be brave enough to unlearn. Unlearning requires one to detox oneself from the toxins of mediocrity injected through the averaging and cutting off of one's unique edges, thus resulting in the deformity of one's dimensions.

You have to unlearn by cultivating an inquisitive mind and an attitude of critical inquiry. Doubt everything until you can prove it. Be slow to say, "I believe," instead, be comfortable saying, "I do not know, yet." Yes, "I DO NOT KNOW, YET."

The moment you state, "I believe" is the very moment you instruct your mind to veer off and deviate from its inquisitive nature.

A mind that has lost its essence of inquisitiveness is a dull mind, a dead mind, a drone's mind, a slave's mind, yes, a mind that waits to be controlled and manipulated by some other master being.

Do not be a dull mind. Say NO to "I believe." Let this be the first thing to unlearn.

RE-LEARN

The process of relearning involves mindfulness. One has to be aware of the nature of being and the nature of things. One has to become an independent observer (not one employing tainted lenses, toxic knowledge, and crooked instruments).

In this re-learning process, after being aware, one has to practice experiential learning. In experiential learning, the main objective is to discover the truth. Truth can only be discovered through experiencing it, not through book knowledge, beliefs, traditions, and assumptions.

The grand purpose of re-learning is recasting your real dimensions so that you can fit into your life's jigsaw puzzle.

Re-learning involves inquisitiveness, critical inquiry, and re-creating your vision.

Re-learning involves re-image-nation, yes, repopulating the pixels of your vision based on your very own experiential learning, not someone else's indoctrination.

Success is your ability to unlearn the old and re-learn anew.

I AM WHO I SAY I AM

One important lesson to learn is that to be a master does not necessarily mean to wield crude power. A lot of us have the misconception that masters must wield political or financial power over us. Jesus did not, yet he was called "master."

According to ancient teachings, wisdom tempered with humility was one of his great qualities. Being fair and just was another great quality. Ultimately, to be loving and forgiving.

Ancient wisdom taught people how to be loving and forgiving. Neither of these two qualities can exist without the other.

A great master is one who loves unconditionally and forgives without being prodded to do so. Why?

In forgiving, you stop becoming a slave to someone else's behavior. You free yourself from being burdened by that person. There is simply no way you can be a master if you are a slave to someone else.

In loving, you appreciate that some people's behavior, however harmful it may seem to be, is an opportunity for you to rise above them.

When you do not give way to hating, to discriminating, to grudges, then the buds of love start growing in the garden of your mind. Eventually, you become the master of the garden and the fruits that abound.

To become a master, you must, first of all, realize that nothing in this world is real. Everything is just an illusion. And like all illusions, everything has an end.

To become a master, you must also realize that the meaning of everything is that which you give it. Do not ever think that any other person has the same sense of the thing that you are experiencing. Experience is as unique as your fingerprint. What you experience is what you perceive, no one else has the knowledge, the power, or audacity to claim otherwise.

Lastly, to become a master, you must realize that "I am who I say I am" holds true.

CHAPTER TEN

HAPPINESS!??

Happiness! One of the most sold-out packages in the capitalist market today. Many advertisements disguisedly show us the standard of happiness. Yet, like in any capitalist market, some cues associate this "happiness" product with material prowess.

The subtle message from the capitalistic marketers is that you can buy happiness. That there is a market for it, and all that you need is to afford its price tag.

So, what is the price of happiness?

Where is that market where one can buy happiness?

Do you think a Ferrari or a massive mansion will make you happy?

And if it is material prowess that brings this happiness, why do we have statistics that seem to show that those in the wealthiest countries have the highest prevalence of suicide and psychological illness?

Happiness blesses those who can tell the difference between what is essential and what isn't.

A professor stood before his philosophy class and had some items in front of him. When the class began, wordlessly, he picked up a very large and empty jar and proceeded to fill it with golf balls.

He then asked the students if the jar was full. They agreed that it was. So, the professor then picked up a box of small pebbles and poured them into the jar. He shook the jar lightly. The pebbles rolled into the open areas between the golf balls. He then asked the students again if the jar was full. They agreed it was.

The professor next picked up a box of sand and poured it into the jar. Of course, the sand filled up everything else. He asked once more if the jar was full. The students responded with a unanimous "Yes." The professor then produced two cans of beer from under the table and poured the entire contents into the jar, effectively filling the empty space between the sand. The students laughed.

"Now," said the professor, as the laughter subsided, "I want you to recognize that this jar represents your life. The golf balls are the important things—your family, your children, your health, your friends, your favorite passions—things that, if everything else was lost and only they remained, your life would still be full. The pebbles are the other things that matter like your job, your house, your car.

The sand is everything else—the small stuff. If you put the sand into the jar first" he continued, "there is no room for the pebbles or the golf balls. The same goes for life. If you spend all your time and energy on the small stuff, you will never have room for the things that are important to you.

Pay attention to the things that are critical to your happiness. Play with your children. Take time to get medical checkups. Take your partner out to dinner. There will always be time to clean the house, and fix the rubbish. Take care of the golf balls first, the things that really matter. Set your priorities. The rest is just sand."

One of the students raised her hand and inquired what the beer represented. The professor smiled. "I'm glad you asked. It just goes to show you that, no matter how full your life may seem, there's always room for a couple of beers."

More often than not, we seek old wisdom from people who lived millenniums ago. We imagine how happy they were. We try to follow their wisdom to be happy. We trace this wisdom in religions, old scripture, and indigenous peoples' traditions.

Yet, what we forget is the contribution of the environment to this happiness. Our ancestors were not threatened by carbon emissions; they were not threatened by all kinds of cancer due to consuming synthetic substances. They were closer to nature than we are.

When you look at their lifestyle, they did not disturb the balance of nature. They harmoniously existed with nature. They simply let nature be, only doing that which was necessary for their survival.

If nature provokes you with a disease, yes, you can respond to that provocation by finding a cure. But, if it has not, why unnecessarily consume drugs, such as muscle enhancing drugs, penile enhancing drugs, virginity drugs, and others? Why can't you simply let your nature be?

The most significant cause of loss of happiness is unnecessary provocations to nature, thus destroying its balance and harmony. When nature is unbalanced and lacks harmony, it will respond in ways that will not grant you peace and serenity. Consider earthquakes, landslides, storms, floods, etc., that result from human destruction of the ecosystem. Nature's fury is mighty and is no respecter of human boundaries.

To LET IT BE is to not care about those things that do not add value to your well-being. It is to keep off unnecessary distractions.

Happiness is that beautiful pool in a mirage. Whenever there is a flat shiny surface during a burst of bright sunshine, chances are high that you are likely going to see a beautiful mirage. This mirage may appear as one of the clearest, cleanest, and most calming pools.

It is enough just to entertain your imagination and be happy that you are a witness to it while the sunshine still lasts.

However, if you attempt to go swim in this pool, it either moves farther away or simply disappears. This is when ghosts of sorrow may decide to prey on your curiosity. You not only miss the pool, but your urge to dive and swim in it increases. You are left tormented by something that you thought existed.

There are many mirages in life. The secret to happiness is to identify them and simply leave them to the entertainment of your imagination.

Excessive alcohol, abundant sex, superfluous beauty, vacuous heroism, fame, and power, are common mirages. Many people have pursued them and ended up more miserable than they were before they embarked on such pursuits. In moderation, some of these things undoubtedly make us happy. But when we overindulge in them, when we become so attached to them such that it becomes painfully unbearable to detach, then they become our source of misery rather than happiness.

Stop pursuing happiness, and it will rest with you. Happiness is like a shadow (or a mirage)—the more you pursue it, the more it runs away, you have to learn to let it be and admire it in its very form.

WILL HAPPINESS GIVE A DAMN ABOUT YOU?

An old man lived in the village. The whole village was tired of him; he was always gloomy, he constantly complained, and was always in a bad mood. The longer he lived, the viler he became, and the more poisonous were his words. People did their best to avoid him because his misfortune was contagious. He created the feeling of unhappiness in others.

But one day, when he turned eighty, an incredible thing happened. Instantly everyone started hearing the rumor: "The old man is happy today, he doesn't complain about anything, smiles, and even his face is freshened up."

The whole village gathered around the man and asked him, "What happened to you?"

The old man replied, "Nothing special. Eighty years I've been chasing happiness, and it was useless. And then I decided to live without happiness and just enjoy life. That's why I'm happy now."

Happiness is about not thinking about it. When you think a lot about happiness, it stops caring about you. But the moment you stop thinking about it, is the very moment it starts caring about you.

Happiness comes when you LET IT BE! If you keep pursuing happiness, you simply will not get it.

Once Buddha was walking from one town to another town with a few of his followers. While they were travelling, they happened to pass a lake. They stopped there and Buddha told one of his disciples, I am thirsty. Do get me some water from that lake there.

The disciple walked up to the lake. When he reached it, he noticed that some people were washing clothes in the water and, right at that moment, a bullock cart started crossing through the lake. As a result, the water became very muddy, very turbid. The disciple thought, How can I give this muddy water to Buddha to drink! So, he came back and told Buddha, the water in there is very muddy. I don't think it is fit to drink.

After about half an hour, again Buddha asked the same disciple to go back to the lake and get him some water to drink. The disciple obediently went back to the lake. This time he found that the lake had absolutely clear water in it. The mud had settled down and the water above it looked fit to be had. So, he collected some water in a pot and brought it to Buddha.

Buddha looked at the water, and then he looked up at the disciple and said,

> "See what you did to make the water clean. You let it be..
> .. and the mud settled down on its own and you got clear
> water... Your mind is also like that. When it is disturbed,
> just let it be. Give it a little time. It will settle down on its
> own. You don't have to put in any effort to calm it down.
> It will happen. It is effortless. "

What did Buddha emphasize here? He said, It is effortless. Having "peace of mind" is not a strenuous job; it is an effortless process. When there is peace inside you, that peace permeates to the outside. It spreads around you and in the environment, such that people around start feeling that peace and grace.

Happiness is like still water in a muddy pond. We know what happens when you stir a muddy pond: the water gets unsettled and mixes with the mud and other particles that had rested on the bed.

Your vigorous vibrations send shockwaves, which stir the pond and disturb its stillness. The end result is enraged energy that disorients the restful particles.

Again, remember that achieving happiness resembles tranquil water in a pond. Make the least possible disturbance to the nature of being.

The same happens in life. Do not disturb your stillness if you desire happiness. In essence, this is disturbing the restful nature of being.

Every action has a reaction. Disturbing the nature of being creates a reaction. What is important is for you to determine the purpose of this reaction. If you want to draw muddy water, please disturb the pond, stir unrest! However, if you want to draw from its stillness, then do not stir unrest.

Probably, it could be easy to fathom how to achieve happiness, success, and optimism through positive thinking. Of course, there are many different ways. Each one can illustrate unique ways to achieve this. There is no monopoly of means.

Identify negative thoughts

Many people practice negative thinking and negative self-talk without even realizing that they are engaging in them. The best way to tell whether you are engaging in a negative thought or negative self-talk is to check on some common forms of them as listed hereunder:

Filtering—in filtering, you tend to filter off the positive aspects of a situation while magnifying its negative aspects.

Polarizing—in polarizing, you see things as two-dimensional: black or white, good or bad. You do not see the beauty of the middle ground or that which is in between these two polarities. In polarizing, you see people as friends or enemies, results as either perfect success or total failure, a feeling as either absolute love or absolute hate.

Personalizing—this occurs whereby you unnecessarily apportion blame to yourself for happenings that are not within your control.

Catastrophizing—with this kind of thinking, you automatically anticipate the worst outcome of a situation.

The following situations can help you distinguish negative thinking from positive thinking:

A. Before a New Task

Negative thought: I do not think I can do this.

Positive thinking: this is a good chance for new lessons.

B. Before a Difficult Assignment

Negative thinking: this is too complex for me to do.

Positive thinking: I will have to deal with this in an alternative way.

C. If There Is a Lack of Sufficient Resources to Carry Out the Desired Venture

Negative thinking: I cannot do this. I don't have enough resources to make it successful

Positive thinking: necessity is the mother of invention. I will have to give it my best.

D. Extra Work

Negative thinking: this is too much for me to do.

Positive thinking: I have to see how to fit this into my priorities.

E. Work That Seems Impossible to Do

Negative thinking: there is no way this can be done.

Positive thinking: I have to find different approaches to see how it can be done.

F. Proposed Changes to the Way Things Are Done

Negative thinking: this is too radical to be implemented.

Positive thinking: let me seize the moment.

G. Broken Communication

Negative thinking: people avoid talking to me.

Positive thinking: I will see how I can unclog communication channels.

H. Things Are Not Going the Way They Are Supposed To

Negative thinking: nothing is going to change. I give up.

Positive thinking: I have to keep finding better ways to accomplish things.

While it may seem hard to get over negative thoughts, it is possible. Science and practice have proven the profound impact of altering one's thoughts through meditation, mindfulness, and positive affirmations. Millions and millions of people around the world do pray almost on a daily basis.

While there are religious beliefs about prayers, scientific evidence proves that prayers can help relieve one's stress and even alter one's perception of reality. The bulk of prayers involve meditation, mindfulness, and, more importantly—positive affirmation.

Meditation, especially mindfulness meditation, has been found to significantly cut down on negative thoughts. Combined with positive affirmations, this becomes a formidable remedy to persistent negative thoughts.

Practice mindfulness. Mindfulness is being conscious of the present moment. More often than not, negative thoughts derive their roots in the past. Past experiences, negative beliefs, and traditions become a fertile ground for negative thoughts to grow and strengthen.

Mindfulness helps you to detach yourself from the past, thus removing the ground to which negative thoughts are anchored.

Another cause of negative thoughts is fear of the future. While the past brings regrets and resentments, fear of the future breeds worries and anxiety, which lowers one's self-esteem and self-confidence. Loss of self-esteem and self-confidence breeds negative thoughts. Mindfulness helps to stop this fear, anxiety, and worry about the future by focusing on the present.

Positive affirmations blended with meditation and mindfulness can be such a powerful remedy for negative thoughts.

Amplify positive thoughts through affirmations. The best way to do this is through faith and action. You can enhance faith through affirmative prayers and your actions through affirmative action.

Take deliberate affirmative actions. Your actions reinforce your thoughts. The best way to overcome inertia is to act. When you think that it is impossible or you are not capable of doing it, that is the very moment to challenge the thought and act.

Once you act, positive signals are triggered in your brain that counter the negative thoughts and help dispel them. It also helps to boost your faith and confidence that things can be done. It enables you to dismantle the habit of negative thoughts.

LEARN

Some people have faced apparently insurmountable situations but made it, thanks to their positive thinking. These are people who, considering their circumstances, would have otherwise been expected to have given up, failed, or lived in misery. Contrary to expectations, they defied all odds and rose to the top of things. These are people who provide precious lessons on how they made it through positive thinking.

You can look around. You will find that particular person or a group of people who inspire you. If you investigate, you will find that they had challenges that would have otherwise derailed them had they not developed extra-ordinary attitudes and a passion for overcoming the challenges.

History is full of individuals who overcame difficulties through positive thinking so as to achieve milestones that others can only consider miraculous.

Books have been written about them—read them. This way, you will be able to explore and discover the unique traits that rest hidden within them. You will ultimately find out that these traits reflect the positive state of their minds. Learn, be inspired. Practice!

SHARE

There is nothing that prepares you for the best more than sharing. When you share tasks or ideas, new perspectives open up so that you are able to see things with much better clarity. You are able to harness creative energies from different beings. This makes your endeavor a potentially more successful one.

You can share your positive thoughts and actions with others through forums, seminars, webinars, discussion groups, social clubs, and charity ventures. You can also share positive thoughts through writing.

The good thing about technology is that it has enabled us to interact wherever we are. Besides physical forums, which sometimes can be challenging to organize in view of prohibitive costs and time, we now have electronic forums, webinars, and discussion boards where you can share your positive thoughts and get more honest and genuine responses. Of course, this will never be the best replacement for face-to-face interactions, but in the absence of that, this becomes the second-best option.

While technology exists for us to interact, it cannot replace the warm aura and immediacy of human encounters. There are those attributes that technology cannot effectively transmit, such as a great handshake, a pat on the back, a hug, or the radiance of a warm, hearty smile. These are things that can only be experienced physically through a face-to-face encounter.

Thus, it is imperative, whenever possible, to form or belong to social groups and clubs where you can share your positive thoughts to inspire others and get inspired in return. This is the best way your positive thoughts get amplified.

Charity work is one of those activities where like-minded people get together voluntarily to carry out a cause that benefits others. Not every person can volunteer his or her free time to charity causes. It takes a few determined souls to do this. A critical attribute of those people who love carrying out this kind of assistance is that they have an inordinately high degree of positive thinking. They are simply inspired to go against all the odds to see that they deliberately participate in uplifting the well-being of others, thus collectively raising the level of humanity for all.

When you volunteer your time, you will most likely meet a group of positive thinkers. You sharpen their positive thinking as you too get sharpened. You learn as you teach. You both practice your thoughts. This is one of the best ways to uplift your attitude.

Reading content on positive thinking, such as this book, can significantly inspire and reinforce your goals. However, this is passive. You are merely receiving without giving. The best way is to read and write. You can write articles, poems, and blog posts about positive thinking.

EXUDE COMPASSION

Compassion is a compelling willingness to serve others to boost their well-being. Compassion chiefly concerns itself with helping others in such a way that can alleviate their suffering and uplift them.

Compassion is devoid of competition, a game of negative thought that seeks to divide and discriminate. Empathy is a positive emotion that sees all humankind as deserving good.

Whenever you engage in acts of compassion, your prejudices (consequences of negative thoughts about others) naturally dissolve and become neutralized. You only see human beings—not races, not colors, not languages, not ethnicities, not classes, not religions, not nationalities or other kinds of divisions and discriminations that cause people to compete against each other, resulting in many forms of suffering including poverty, slavery, and wars. With compassion, all these prejudices naturally dissolve.

Once a group of fifty people was attending a seminar.

Suddenly the speaker stopped and started giving each person a balloon. Each one was asked to write his/her name on it using a marker pen. Then all the balloons were collected and put in another room.

Now these delegates were let in that room and asked to find the balloon which had their name written, within five minutes.

Everyone was frantically searching for their name, pushing, colliding with each other, and there was utter chaos.

At the end of five minutes, no one could find their own balloon.

Now, each one was asked to randomly collect a balloon and give it to the person whose name was written on it. Within minutes everyone had their own balloon.

The speaker began: This is exactly what is happening in our lives. Everyone is frantically looking for happiness all around, not knowing where it is. Our happiness lies in the happiness of other people. Give them their happiness, you will get your own happiness. And this is the purpose of human life.

Compassion is the highest essence of positive thinking. It is a consequence of a purified positive thought—a thought distilled from all human biases and prejudices. It is both a real and an ideal state. It is real in the sense that it can be achieved and ideal in the sense that its potential has no definite end. Yes, it is an eternity in itself.

The people who are remembered most for their significant positive deeds are people who had compassion. Yes, those who thought positively about the need to rise above negativities—biases, and prejudices; to bring together and mend the torn garment of humanity.

Compassion is not such a complicated thing to strive for. It is one of the most straightforward steps one can begin with. It is inherent in human nature, but we lose it through our cultural biases and an educational system that emphasizes competition and the hoarding of goods and services so that we may get higher earnings.

Compassion is simply getting back to the basics, exploring your inner value that has been muted by the complexities of modernity and compelled into the pursuit of monetary gain.

The commercialization of "compassion" has made many people fear it. It has led many people to think that you have to be extremely wealthy or a celebrity to start committing to acts of compassion. This is pure commercialization.

You do not have to make millions or billions to carry out acts of compassion. You do not have to become a celebrity. You do not have to become that "important" person in society before you start practicing compassion. That is not compassion but simply a kind of publicity arising from seeking personal gain.

Compassion is the bond that unites all humanity. Positive thinking can enable you to achieve this bond.

SEEK REVOLUTION

When most people hear about revolution, they imagine wars, chaos, blood, death, and other violent catastrophes that come about due to political conflict. Revolution does not have to be violent.

Revolution is simply about a complete shift in the way things are done. It is an entirely new way of doing things. It is about tapping into the ever-fresh creative energies within you and utilizing them to transform yourself and others.

No revolution can be achieved without optimized positive thinking. A continuous, persistent, and deliberate effort at positive thinking connects one to the creative energy flowing within. This is a mighty river that silently runs within each and every human being.

Unfortunately, when our mind is hijacked through patterns imposed by education, cultural conditioning, and established traditions, it becomes stale and lost. It seeks to move along these maps created by others and imposed on us by others.

It is through positive thinking and self-awareness that we realize we have these mind maps imposed on us. It is through positive thinking that one decides to find a way out of this maze of mind maps. One can easily feel derailed if going outside one's comfort zone. But, with persistence, one gets away from traps of enslavement and onto the path of liberty and creativity.

It is by stepping outside of these limiting beliefs that one truly becomes a revolutionary—one who has created their own path; one who has found the mighty river of creativity flowing within; one who is capable of drawing water from this river of creativity and is thus able to quench their thirst—a thirst for knowing one's purpose in life and for feeling a powerful connection to his fellow beings.

When you actualize positive thinking through compassion, you are ever optimistic about your power to do good deeds. You trust your inner strength to reconnect with the rest of humanity. You are ever conscious of the well-being of others as your ultimate responsibility.

Every person that rises up from disaster, calamity, and adversity due to your effort becomes a source of success, joy, and happiness. Every radiating pleasure experienced by others due to your positive aura and sense of inspiration excites in you more optimism, a sense of success and happiness.

Positive thinking is celebrated. It liberates you. But, positive thinking actualized through compassion liberates not only you but all of humanity. Every step and every technique geared toward achieving positive thinking should engender the feeling of what humanity could become in a fully compassionate world—a heaven on earth! Small steps—step by step, persistently committed toward this end, can truly transform this world.

LIFE!

It can be shared forever, but cannot be kept forever. When given to another, it brings great joy to all; when taken, the anguish for many is great.

It is sometimes maintained by less than a thread and sometimes lost despite the hope of millions.

Its frailty and end are apparent, but its strength and limits endless.

Share your life with others so they may have more joy.

When this life is over, let the meaning of our lives be found not on a list of accomplishments, but in the hearts and souls of the people with whom we shared our fragile existence.

Let our lives not be measured so much by what we did for others, but by what we helped people do for themselves.

We fear death. It is human to do so. However, looking at it keenly, it is the fear of physical pain and the fear of loss of attachment to what we hold dear that causes this fear.

Yet, you go to bed; you can never sleep, not until your mind moves away from attachment to thoughts and everything that you hold dear.

Therefore, we experience some form of dying every time we are seized by sleep. Yet, most of the time, when we wake up, we feel refreshed and rejuvenated; even if we don't, it is still better than if we never fell asleep.

In sleeping, we surrender our attachments so this process of renewal and regeneration can take place. Why not extend this surrender of attachment to our wakeful moments?

Sometimes we do surrender our attachments, but not often. A parent partially surrenders their son or daughter in marriage. All parents partially surrender their children when they attain adulthood so that they may become more independent and productive.

Parents know that this is the best way for their sons and daughters to fully optimize their potential, to become happier, and flourish. They, too, were surrendered to become who they became—parents.

The best love you can express is to let go. If you detain a dove in a cage so that it does not fly, you do not love it. You are not expressing love to it, only cruelty. The same is the case when you unreasonably detain animals in a zoo. You not only deny them freedom but your love. How can they be happy?

Happiness is to let go. It is to die off each and every moment. In this dying, you let that magnetic bundle of attachment release. It is like switching off electric energy from an electromagnet.

Giving a damn is simply to remain attached to that which ought to die. That is not an expression of love. It is still cruelty. In essence, you are controlling it, manipulating it, limiting it, and obstructing it. Let go of it so that its energy bundle can flow to another direction; after all, there is no destruction but transformation.

When holding onto something brings you more loss, pain, and suffering than letting go of it, then prudence dictates that it is time to let go. Die-off from it.

LEAVING NO TRACE

People struggle in life to leave a trace, be it a legacy, a bequeathing of property, children, or whatever they think will be used to remember them. In this struggle to leave a trace, they toil and suspend their very own moment of happiness. While the trace is left, it is not always as they desired.

One great lesson we ought to learn from swimming is that, when you cling to water, you will sink like a stone and drown. However, when you set yourself free from clinging, you will be able to swim and float.

Attachments are like clinging. The more you cling to that which no longer serves your highest being, the more you lower yourself.

In your lowest state, you drown and wallow in the miasma of anger, hate, desperation, and ill will.

While we interact with people, we have to guard against leaving negative traces in their lives. We have to be mindful of our actions, words, and expressions.

When you dislike the unpleasant things that other people do, you are likely to react, and this reaction leaves a trace. For example, someone says nasty things about you, and then you get angry and insult the person. Those insults will register in that person's mind. You will not have a chance to erase them. You have no control over that person's mind register. However, if you minded your own business and walked away, there would not be such a trace.

If you cannot afford to be misunderstood, then for goodness' sake, don't do anything new or innovative.

Though pursuing a new or innovative idea will be hard, follow your passion, and be proud of your choice.

The great thing about humans in general is we're always improving things. And so invincible individuals need to follow their curiosity and follow their passions.

CONCLUSION

Life is a bundle of energy, and it is the interaction and transformation of this energy that creates our reality. By changing the nature of this transformation, we can create a new frame and fill it with the picture of the reality that we would love to see.

Power is energy in action. You have to harness this power to enlighten your mind. Moreover, you can use this power of the invincible mind, not only to transform yourself but those around you. And with this power, you can change future generations by slowly and gradually altering the genetic map from which they are created.

We can free our minds from so many sources of weak judgments—including traditions, taboos, beliefs, habits, unfounded knowledge, and lessons of our past experiences, among others.

This book is a bold endeavor to share with you my little secrets gained from my experience on the journey to crack the code to my mind. There is no doubt that this is a life-long journey, and I am still arriving. I am still a traveler.

I would like you to join me on this journey so that together we can form a companionship of invincible minds, and if that happens and continues to happen, we will be able to form a community of invincible minds. And from communities, we can create societies and, eventually, a whole world. It all begins with a single step.

An invincible mind is not just about you. It is also about others—both born and yet to be born. This is the only worthy heritage that you can bequeath to generations to come—a lasting inspiration, forever energized.

The invincible mind is not arrogant. The invincible mind is not careless. The invincible mind is not a "self-centered" or "egoistic" mind.

The invincible mind is simply that mind that accepts its naked being. The invincible mind is one unencumbered by the limitations of the past. The invincible mind is free from the trappings of attachment. The invincible mind does not find comfort in scapegoating and escapism.

An invincible mind knows that it has the power to find solutions to every challenge, and as such, whenever solutions are not found, it takes responsibility for its shortcomings. Yet, it does not blame itself or condemn itself as a failure. It knows, just like in a race, some solutions require a sprint while others require a marathon to accomplish.

The invincible mind has the power to attract and repel, attach and detach without being adulterated by fear considerations.

The invincible mind does not limit itself to what it can inquire about. There is simply no taboo to an inquiry.

The invincible mind does not deliberately bury itself in the darkness of traditions and beliefs. It consciously seeks to tear itself from the societal garment and free itself from this garment's limitation

Giving not a damn is boldness. It is bravery. It is taking responsibility for yourself. It is the absence of fear.

Whenever there is arrogance, there rests fear; fear of succumbing to the disarming truth and the fear of humility.

Whenever there is arrogance, there is a weak mind with a selfish ego. It is commonly said that arrogance comes before a fall. Arrogance blinds you from seeing, from being prudent, from being cautious, from being rational, and from being judicious.

The pain of hurt from the fall is simply a symptom. The real disease is ignorance. Selfish ego is a manifestation of this ignorance. Until you heal your wounded mind, arrogance will remain its symptom.

An invincible mind is a healing mind, not an injuring mind. An invincible mind has a conscience. It does not seek to hurt, for seeking to hurt others is, in essence, seeking to injure their nakedness. Be free and free others up.

Don't give a damn!

Shake it off and step up!

Good Luck!

THANKS

Thank you for reading my book. If you enjoyed it, won't you please take a moment to leave a book review at your favorite retailer?

If someone you care about is looking to improve the quality of their life, or struggling with any issue including stress, anxiety, self-hate, or lack of self-confidence, please tell them about this book.

***

Whenever you buy my book, 1% of the profit will be donated to Cancer and Heart Associations.

With each donation, together, we will live in a world where no child or family fear cancer or heart disease.

It's one of the most cost-effective ways to extend life and fulfills my biggest mission, which is to spread healthy habits and help others realize their full potential.

Alex Neumann

ABOUT THE AUTHOR

Alex Neumann is an author, engineer, corporate mentor, and technology investor. He is a member of The Independent Book Publishers Association.

He holds a Bachelor of Arts in English Literature. Also, he holds Bachelor's and Master's degrees in Computer Science.

Alex lives with his wife, dog, and cat. He enjoys good wine and catching sun rays with his lazy dog.

Ever since childhood, he has been interested in understanding how some people are able to thrive through challenging times in life, and he hopes that by sharing these hard-fought lessons with each other, we can make this world a better place.

Connect with me and subscribe to my blog to be notified of frequent giveaways, free chapters, blog posts, new releases, and pre-release specials.

www.alexneumann.co

facebook.com/alexneumannco

instagram.com/alexneumannco

twitter.com/alexneumannco

Made in the USA
Columbia, SC
30 January 2021